Beacon Small-Group Bible Studies

Acts, Part 2

Beacon Small-Group Bible Studies

ACTS

(Part 2: Chapters 13—28)

The Continuing Mission of the Church

by

LeBron Fairbanks

Beacon Hill Press of Kansas City
Kansas City, Missouri

Acknowledgment

Throughout these Bible studies, quotations are included from the writings of Dr. William M. Greathouse, general superintendent of the Church of the Nazarene. From 1955 to 1976, in the *Adult Bible Teacher/Bible School Journal,* Dr. Greathouse wrote the column "Toward Christian Living," from which these quotations are taken.

Permission to quote from the following copyrighted versions of Bible is acknowledged with appreciation:

The Holy Bible, New International Version (NIV), copyright © 1978 by the New York International Bible Society.

Good News Bible, Today's English Version (TEV)—Old Testament © American Bible Society, 1976; New Testament © American Bible Society, 1966, 1971, 1976.

New English Bible (NEB), © The Delegates of the Oxford University Press and The Syndics of the Cambridge University Press, 1961, 1970.

New American Standard Bible (NASB), © The Lockman Foundation, 1960, 1962, 1963, 1968, 1971, 1972, 1973, 1975, 1977.

Contents

HOW TO USE THIS STUDY GUIDE

Before You Begin This Adventure in a
Small-Group Bible Study . . .
Read These Pages of Introduction

God has created us with a basic human need for close personal relationships. This may take place *as you gather in a small group* to apply the Bible to your life.

I. What Should Happen in Small-Group Bible Study?

"They devoted themselves to the apostles' teaching and to the fellowship . . . and to prayer" (Acts 2:42, NIV).

Each group is different . . . yet all should include three kinds of activity—
DISCUSSION BIBLE STUDY
SHARING EXPERIENCES
PRAYING TOGETHER

The time you spend in Bible study, sharing, and praying will vary according to the needs of the group. However, do not neglect any of these activities.

The Bible contains God's plan for our salvation and gives us His guidance for our lives. Keep the focus on God speaking to you from His Word.

On the other hand, just to learn Bible facts will make little difference in a person's life. To give opportunity for persons to *share* what the truth means to them is to let God come alive today. Learn to listen intently to others and to share what you feel God's Word is saying to you.

Allow time for *prayer*. Personal communion with God is essential in all fruitful Bible studies. Determine to make prayer more than a "nod to God" at the beginning or end of each session. As members participate in sincere, unhurried prayer—you will be amazed how God's power will meet needs in your group . . . today!

II. How to Begin Your First Session Together

The leader of a new group may wish to prepare name tags with first and last names large enough to be seen plainly.

It is important to order the *Beacon Small-Group Bible Study* guides and give one to each person in your group at the beginning of the first session. Pass out the guides and refer the group to this section of the introductory guidance. Then ask each person to consider the following:

One thing I would like to gain from sharing in this time together is:

Rank the following in order using the number one to indicate the most important and the number five the least important.

( ) 1. Learning to know Bible truths and apply them to my life.
( ) 2. A chance to begin all over again in my spiritual life.
( ) 3. To grow in my personal faith in God.
( ) 4. To deepen my friendships with others in the group as we study the Word together.
( ) 5. Other purpose _____

Take time to go around the group to introduce yourselves. Then let each member share what he would like to gain from this Bible study by filling in the blanks and by discussing this statement: I chose _____ as number one because _____. I put _____ as number five because _____.

At this point, pause for prayer, asking God to bless this Bible study and especially to meet the needs just expressed by the members of the group.

III. A Key to Success . . . Make a Group Commitment

What should be included in the group commitment? At the first or second meeting, read the following points, then discuss each one separately.

1. Agree to make regular attendance a top priority of the group. Commitment to each other is of vital importance.

2. Where and when will the group meet?
   Decide on a place and time. The place can be always in the same home or in a different home each week, at a restaurant, or in any other relaxed setting. Plan to be on time.

   The time _____ the place(s) _____
   How often?   ( ) Every week
                     ( ) Every other week

3. Decide on the length of the meetings.
   The minimum should be one hour—maximum two hours. Whatever you decide, be sure to dismiss on time. Those who wish may remain after the group is dismissed. Length _____.

4. Decide whether the same person will lead each session, or if you prefer a group coordinator and a rotation of leaders.

   Our leader or coordinator is _____.

5. Agree together that there shall be no criticism of others. Also no discussion of church problems, and no gossip shall be expressed in the group. Our goal in this Bible study is to affirm and to build up each other.

6. Decide on the maximum number of people your group should contain. When this maximum is reached, you will encourage the formation of a new group. We want our group to grow. Newcomers, as they understand and agree to the group commitment, will keep things fresh. Feel free to

bring a friend. Whenever our group reaches an average attendance of
_____ persons for three consecutive weeks, we will plan to begin a new
group.

Do not become a closed clique. This would eventually lead to an ingrown
group. Our goal is outreach, friendliness, and openness to new people.

7. Our time together as a group will be more fulfilling if all of us complete our
personal Bible reading before we come together again.

Are group members deciding to make this commitment to personal Bible reading and reflection? _____

8. Decide on the number of times you wish to meet before you reevaluate the
areas of your commitment. (Enter below.)

MY COMMITMENT TO CHRIST
AND THE MEMBERS OF MY GROUP

I agree to meet with others in my group for _____ weeks to
become a learner in God's Word.

I commit myself to give priority to our group gatherings, to a
thoughtful reading of the Bible passages to be explored,
and to love and support others in my group.

Signed _____ Date _____

IV. Guidelines

1. Get acquainted with each other; be on a first-name basis.

2. Each one bring your Bible and keep it open during the study.

3. As you read the Bible passage, each person may ask himself three questions: —What does the passage say?
                             —What does it mean?
                             —What does it mean to me?

4. Stay with the Bible passage before you. Moving to numerous cross-ref-
   erences may confuse a person new to the Bible.

5. Avoid technical theological words. Make sure any theological terms you use
   are explained clearly to the group.

6. The leader or coordinator should prepare for each session by studying the
   passage thoroughly before the group meeting, including reviewing the

questions in the study guide. In the group study, the leader should ask the study guide questions, giving adequate time for the discussion of each question.

Remember, the leader is not to lecture on what he has learned from studying, but should lead the group in discovering for themselves what the scripture says. In sharing your discoveries say, "The Scripture says . . . ," rather than, "My church says . . ."

7. The leader should not talk too much and should not answer his own questions. The leader should give opportunity for anyone who wishes to speak. Redirect some of the questions back to the group. As members get to know each other better, the discussion will move more freely.

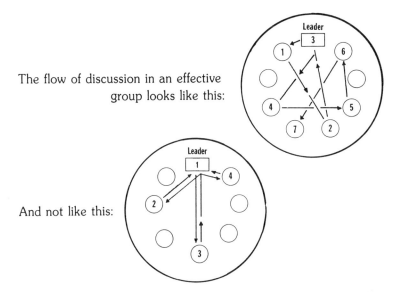

The flow of discussion in an effective group looks like this:

And not like this:

8. In a loving but firm manner maintain the guidelines for the group. Discourage overtalkative members from monopolizing the time. If necessary, the leader may speak privately to the overtalkative one and enlist his aid in encouraging all to participate. Direct questions to all persons in the group.

9. Plan to reserve some time at the end of each session for prayer together. Encourage any who wish to lead out in spoken prayer in response to the scripture truths or personal needs expressed in the group.

Even if you do not complete all the study for that particular meeting, *take time to pray.* The main purpose of group Bible study is not just to cover all the facts, but to apply the truth to human lives. It will be exciting to discover your lives growing and changing as you encourage each other in Christ's love.

A highly effective way to pray in a group like this is "conversationally." Conversational prayer includes:

a. Each group member who wishes to do so tells God frankly what he has to say to Him.

b. Praying done in a conversational tone—directly, simply, briefly.

c. Only one thing is prayed about at a time—a personal concern.

d. Once a group member has introduced his concern, at least one other member, and probably several, by audible prayer "covers with love" their friend's concern.

e. Then there is a waiting in silence before God. Each person listens to what God is saying to him.

f. Following the listening period, another member may introduce a personal concern in prayer. The prayer time continues with members feeling free to pray several times.

V. Aids for Your Study

For Group Leaders

You will find helpful, *How to Lead a Small-Group Bible Study*, by Gene Van Note, available from the Beacon Hill Press of Kansas City, Box 527, Kansas City, MO 64141.

For Leaders, Coordinators, and Participants

Bible commentaries should not be taken with you to the study period, but it is often helpful to refer to sound commentaries and expositions in your preparation. We recommend:

> *Beacon Bible Commentary*
> Volume 7—John—Acts
> *Beacon Bible Expositions*
> Volume 5—Acts

It is also helpful to refer occasionally to some general Bible resources, such as:

> *Know Your New Testament*, by Ralph Earle
> *Halley's Bible Handbook*

The above resources are available from Beacon Hill Press of Kansas City or from your publishing house.

—This introduction by Wil M. Spaite

THE CHURCH GOES ABROAD

THE ACTS
Part II
Chapters 13—28

"And ye shall be witnesses unto me . . . unto the uttermost part of the earth" (Acts 1:8).

FIRST MISSIONARY JOURNEY

ANTIOCH in SYRIA (13:1-3)
BARNABAS and SAUL
SENT OUT

SELEUCIA (13:4)

SALAMIS (13:5)

PAPHOS (13:6-12)
SERGIUS PAULUS
CONVERTED
SAUL BECOMES PAUL (v. 9)

PERGA (13:13)
PAUL ASSUMES
LEADERSHIP
MARK RETURNS HOME

ANTIOCH of PISIDIA (13:14-52)
PAUL'S SERMON
GENTILE RESPONSE

ICONIUM (14:1-7)

LYSTRA (14:8-20)
PAUL STONED

DERBE and RETURN (14:21-28)

COUNCIL at JERUSALEM (15:1-34)

SECOND MISSIONARY JOURNEY

ANTIOCH (15:35-40)
PAUL vs. BARNABAS
PAUL and SILAS LEAVE

LYSTRA (16:1-5)
TIMOTHY JOINS PARTY

TROAS (16:6-11)
MACEDONIAN CALL

PHILIPPI (16:12-40)
LYDIA–FIRST CONVERT
JAILER CONVERTED

THESSALONICA (17:1-9)

BEREA (17:10-14)

ATHENS (17:15-34)
SERMON on MARS' HILL

CORINTH (18:1-17)
PRISCILLA and AQUILA
CRISPUS CONVERTED
PAUL before GALLIO

EPHESUS and RETURN (18:18-22)

THIRD MISSIONARY JOURNEY

ANTIOCH (18:23)

GALATIA and PHRYGIA (18:23)

EPHESUS (19:1-41)
EPHESIAN PENTECOST
DEMETRIUS CAUSES RIOT

MACEDONIA (20:1-2)

CORINTH (Greece) (20:2-3)

PHILIPPI (20:3-6)

TROAS (20:6-12)
ALL-NIGHT SERVICE

MILETUS (20:13-38)
FAREWELL to EPHESIAN
ELDERS

TYRE and CAESAREA (21:1-14)

JERUSALEM (21:15-23:31)
ARREST and DEFENSE

CAESAREA (23:31-26:32)
TRIALS and APPEAL

VOYAGE to ROME (27:1-28:16)

ROME (28:17-31)

11

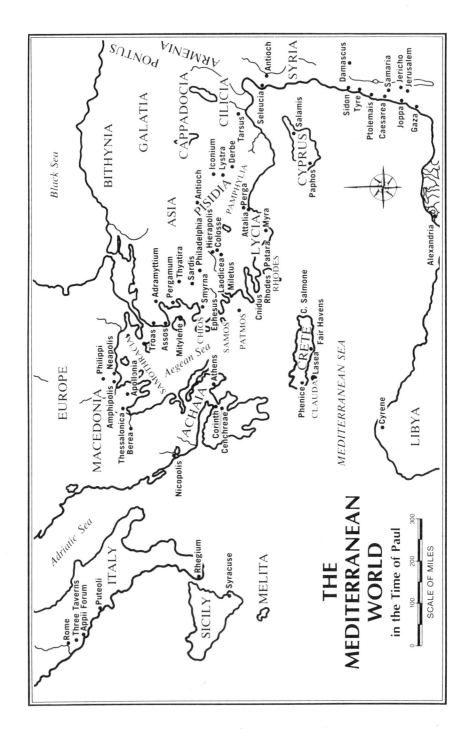

THE
MEDITERRANEAN
WORLD
in the Time of Paul

SCALE OF MILES

0 100 200 300

PONTUS
ARMENIA
SYRIA
Antioch
Damascus
Samaria
Jericho
Jerusalem
Sidon
Tyre
Ptolemais
Caesarea
Joppa
Gaza
Seleucia
BITHYNIA
GALATIA
CAPPADOCIA
CILICIA
Tarsus
CYPRUS
Salamis
Paphos
Black Sea
ASIA
PISIDIA
Iconium
Antioch
Lystra
Derbe
Philadelphia
Hierapolis
Colosse
Laodicea
PAMPHYLIA
Perga
Attalia
LYCIA
Myra
Patara
Rhodes
RHODES
Cnidus
Adramyttium
Pergamum
Thyatira
Sardis
Smyrna
Ephesus
Miletus
PATMOS
SAMOS
CHIOS
Mitylene
Assos
Troas
SAMOTHRACIA
Aegean Sea
C. Salmone
CRETE
Lasea
Fair Havens
Phenice
CLAUDA
MEDITERRANEAN SEA
EUROPE
MACEDONIA
Philippi
Neapolis
Amphipolis
Apollonia
Thessalonica
Berea
ACHAIA
Athens
Corinth
Cenchreae
Nicopolis
Alexandria
Cyrene
LIBYA
Adriatic Sea
ITALY
Rome
Three Taverns
Appii Forum
Puteoli
Rhegium
Syracuse
SICILY
MELITA

12

The Format

Each chapter in this study guide is designed for maximum student involvement. The format for each chapter is as follows:

Introduction—The theme of the Bible passage is presented in an introductory paragraph.

Opening Prayer—A prayer is provided for the beginning of each lesson, focusing on the central theme to be discussed.

Review—This part of each lesson gives opportunity to reflect on what God has done in your life since the last Bible study. The review becomes an integral part of each session.

Scriptural Analysis and Application—The majority of the time together in Bible study is spent analyzing and applying the scriptural truths to one's life. Space is provided to write personal and/or group responses to the discussion questions.

A Reflection—At the conclusion of each session you are asked to identify one insight from the study which stands out. After the significant idea is identified, you are asked to tell how you plan to implement the insight in your life—when, where, or with whom.

Prayer Time—Each session closes with group prayer. The thrust of the experience is "How can the Word be applied to my life this week?" Space is provided in the back of the study guide for an intercessory prayer list, and other specific forms of ministry to be undertaken during the week.

Something to Think About or Do—Suggestions are given each week for further thought and action. These are not formal assignments. Rather, you are encouraged to think about them in the week following the Bible study. Included in this section is a suggested Bible memorization passage.

Each session is designed to take approximately 1½ hours. The sessions can be extended or shortened according to the time available and the needs of the group. Don't be bound to the exact sequencing. Each lesson format is a suggestion—a framework—within which a group can gain rich insights and meaningful dialog.

The concept of journaling may be new to you, perhaps even awkward at first. I encourage you, however, to write down your responses, reflections, prayer concerns, and action plan. Your study of the Bible will be revolutionized when you begin to study the Scripture with pen and paper close by. Use this guide as a start in journaling. I suspect that it will not be the last time you do it!

Introduction to Acts 13—28

Acts 1:8 suggests a threefold outline of the book: (1) The Founding of the Church (1:1—8:3); (2) The Broadening of the Church (8:4—12:25); and (3) The Extension of the Church (13:1—28:31).

This last section, which tells of the spread of the gospel "unto the uttermost part of the earth" (1:8), centers around the missionary activity of Paul, although Barnabas' early leadership is noted. These 12 lessons will trace the missionary thrust of Christianity into the Gentile world. Their aim is to deepen the conviction that the responsibility of the Church today under the guidance of the Spirit is to carry the gospel to the whole world.

This section of Acts is historical, but it contains human drama not found elsewhere in the New Testament. You will laugh and weep as you relate the events and personalities in these chapters.

Throughout our study, the thrust of *The Continuing Mission of the Church* will be driven home in numerous ways. Be open to its message to you.

1 The Initiative Is God's

ACTS 13:1-52

Introduction

In today's lesson we have Paul's only full-length recorded sermon. Imagine that you are in the synagogue congregation in Antioch of Pisidia to hear the visiting rabbi from Palestine. It is a Sabbath morning in the year A.D. 46-47. After the reading of the Torah and a related passage from the prophets, one of the rulers of the synagogue invites Paul to give a word of exhortation. Paul goes to the *bima* (pulpit) and makes a gesture inviting attention. He addresses his words to "men of Israel" (Jews and proselytes) and "ye that fear God" (Gentile God fearers).

At the heart of his message is a strong emphasis upon the Resurrection—a note that characterizes New Testament sermons. For the Early Church every Sunday was Easter.

Opening Prayer

Father, we open our eyes to see, our ears to hear, and our minds to understand the great unity between the Old and New Testaments reflected in our biblical passage today. We need to see the underlying harmony that unites the different parts of the Bible.

Give us a new appreciation of You as the great Initiator—constantly working on our behalf—supremely expressed in Your gift of salvation to us.

With deep reverence we approach this chapter and our study together. In Jesus' name. Amen.

Review

Spend a few minutes recalling your walk with Christ in recent days. Perhaps you could ask: What can I praise God for? Are there answers to prayer? Blessings He has provided? A miracle He has performed?

What do I need to confess to the Father? Have I failed or hurt a fellow believer? Have I knowingly sinned against God? Are there needs in my life for which I should ask the prayers of the group?

What can I share with the group that will build them up in Jesus? Are there spiritual lessons I have learned from God's Word? Has He given me light on a particular issue or passage of Scripture? Were there insights discovered that would support and upbuild the group members in their faith? Use the space below to write your responses.

What the Lord Has Done	My Responses: Praise/Confession/Sharing

Scriptural Analysis and Application
Read 13:1-3

Discuss the implications of these verses.

1. Whose plan was the missionary enterprise of the Church? _____

_____

2. Barnabas was from the island of Cyprus in the Mediterranean; Simeon's Latin name, Niger (the Black), indicates he moved in Roman circles; Lucius came from Cyrene in North Africa; Manaen was an aristocratic Jew who had been brought up in a royal setting; and Saul from Tarsus, in Cilicia, had been educated to be a rabbi. What does this list of Antioch church leaders exemplify?

_____ The love of God for people in all walks of life
_____ The universal appeal of Christ
_____ The unifying influence of Christianity
_____ Respect of persons (discrimination)

3. As the group prayed and fasted, who spoke to them (v. 2)? _____

_____

4. Two of the best men were set aside for the task of world evangelism. Who were they (v. 3)? _____ and _____.
Fascinating, isn't it!

Read 13:4-12

Where did these events take place? On the map locate Seleucia, Cyprus, Salamis, and Paphos. On the chart "The Church Goes Abroad" (p. 11) locate the events of the first missionary journey described in verses 4-12.

Who was the third member of the preaching team (much younger—v. 5)? _____

What false prophet confronted the missionaries (v. 6)? _____
_____

What government leader became interested in the Good News (vv. 7, 12)? _____

On your map and on the chart of the first missionary journey, trace Paul's route from Paphos to Antioch in Pisidia (v. 14).

Why did the missionaries seek out the Jewish synagogue as a basis for their operations? (See Rom. 1:16.)

A Look at Paul's Sermon

This first recorded sermon by the apostle Paul falls into three divisions:

a. *The preparation for Christ's coming* (Read 13:16-22)

Do you think Paul was wise in reciting Israel's history in his sermon in the synagogue? Yes ____ No ____ Why?

Paul declared that the messianic promises of the Old Testament were fulfilled in the coming of Jesus. Do you agree ____ disagree ____?

"The New Testament is in the Old concealed; the Old is in the New revealed." Do you see this truth illustrated in Paul's sermon? Yes ____ No ____ Not sure ____

Some have seen Paul's synagogue sermon as noticeably similar to Stephen's (7:2-53). At your convenience, in your own quiet time, you may wish to make a comparison of these two sermons.

b. *Fulfillment in the death and resurrection of Christ*

The major portion of this part of the sermon is devoted to the Resurrection (vv. 30-37). Note similar messages by Paul: Rom. 1:1-4; 1 Cor. 15:1-4.

Using your favorite translation, write out here 1 Cor. 15:14: ___

_____

_____

c. *Justification through faith in Christ* (Read 13:38-41)

Persons are not justified through keeping the law; they are saved through faith in Jesus Christ. That is why Ray Palmer could write:

> *My faith looks up to Thee,*
> *Thou Lamb of Calvary,*
> *Saviour divine!*
> *Now hear me while I pray;*
> *Take all my guilt away.*
> *Oh, let me from this day*
> *Be wholly Thine!*

In verses 40-41 Paul warns his synagogue audience not to take the way of rejection that was predicted in Hab. 1:5. Do you see that warning as relative to us today? Yes _____ No _____

In about 25 words, summarize Paul's sermon. _____

_____

_____

The Response

(Read 13:42-48)

What is meant by the phrase "continue in the grace of God" (v. 43)?

_____

Why did Paul and Barnabas have to first speak the Word of God to the Jews (v. 46)? _____

What was the Gentiles' response to their inclusion in the plan of salvation (v. 48)? _____

Verse 48 seems to say that the choices men make for or against Christ are a matter of foreordination. In his *Explanatory Notes upon the New Testament,* John Wesley writes:

> St. Luke does not say "foreordained." He is not speaking of what was done from eternity, but of what was then done through the preaching of the gospel. . . . It is as if he had said, They believed, *"whose hearts the Lord opened";* as he expresses it in a clearly parallel place speaking of the same kind of ordination (Acts xvi. 14 & c). The original word is not once used in Scrip-

ture to express eternal predestination of any kind. . . . In a word, the expression properly implies, a present operation of divine grace, working faith in the hearers.[1]

Read 13:49-52

What do you think is the relationship of suffering, persecution, and church growth (v. 49)? Read Phil. 1:12-14. _____

What do you think is meant by shaking "the dust from their feet in protest against them" (v. 51, NIV)? _____

Why and how could the disciples be "filled with joy" as a result of their expulsion from the city? _____

A Pause to Reflect

List below one insight from the session which is most significant to you. How do you plan to implement it into your life-style this week?

Prayer Time

Turn to the section in the back of this study guide entitled "My Ministry of Intercession." This is your personal prayer list.

Spend a few minutes reflecting upon the question "What does the Lord want me to do as a result of this Bible study?" Identify specific people, concerns, and needs that you want to lift to the Father in your continuing ministry of intercession. Return to this list throughout the week.

What witnesses of love and care, what acts of encouragement, or what ministries of service does God want you to do or say? Be specific. Write down the who, where, and how.

As time permits, share some of these items with others in the group before you pray together.

Focusing upon the needs represented on your prayer lists, conclude with group prayer.

Something to Think About or Do

Suggested memory verse for the week—Acts 13:47

Before next week, read Acts 14:1-28, using your favorite translation.

2   The People of God Ministering

ACTS 14:1-28

Introduction

What kind of people ought Christians to be? What qualities of character should enhance followers of Christ?

Study this chapter to find answers to these questions. Read the chapter through, thoughtfully looking for clear pictures of the characters of Paul and Barnabas. Although the apostles were men of "like passions" with you and me (James 5:17) they stood tall and Christlike; we do well to emulate them. They were men "separated unto the gospel" (Rom. 1:1). Yet even you and I are men and women of good news, called to serve in a world growing increasingly sinful.

Ministry is a function of every Christian, not something that only a few persons are called to do. All Christians are ministers, called to exercise their ministries where they work—in the home or on the job.

The Church is "the people of God ministering"—involved with God in reconciling the world to himself. To be effective and productive in that ministry, we must possess some of the Christian qualities of Paul and Barnabas.

Opening Prayer (Repeat it together)

Father, so often we experience conflict between our desire to be effective and our track record of ineffectiveness. When we look at our lives and measure them by Your qualities of Christlikeness, we fall short. Help us to understand the reasons for our ineffectiveness.

Too often we desire to increase in security, recognition, control, beauty, and power. You desire for us to increase in faith, in goodness, in self-control, in perseverance, in godliness, in brotherly kindness, and in love.

Forgive us.

Use this session to draw us back to Your will for our lives and to the priorities to which we have committed ourselves. Let us see again the qual-

ities of character You deem important for Your followers. In Christ's name. Amen.

Review

Spend a few minutes counting your blessings. Look back over the past week with the Lord and reflect upon it. Perhaps you could ask:

What can I praise God for? Answers to prayer? Blessings? Miracles of courage?

What do I need to confess to the Father and/or to the group? Failure? Sin? Hurts?

What can I share with the group that will build them up in Jesus? Lessons learned? Insights gained?

Use the space below to respond; in the left column indicate what the Lord has done. In the right column express your personal response.

What the Lord Has Done	My Responses: Praise/Confession/Sharing

Scriptural Analysis and Application

Read 14:1-6

What words describe the impact of Paul and Barnabas' ministry in Iconium (v. 1)?

Do you think Paul and Barnabas were more interested in being *faithful* or *successful?* _____ Why? _____

What was the key to their perseverance (v. 3)? _____

Trace on the map, p. 12, Paul's journey from Perga to Derbe. See also the places and events listed on the chart of the first missionary journey, p. 11.

Why did the missionaries move on from Iconium (vv. 5-6)? _____

Read 14:7-20

What words describe Paul and Barnabas' ministry in Lystra and Derbe (v. 7)? _____

Whose faith do you think was responsible for the healing (vv. 8-10)? The lame man _____ Paul and Barnabas _____ Both _____ Neither _____

There is a legend in the region of Lystra which formed the background of the incident recorded in verses 11-15a. Jupiter (Zeus) and Mercury (Hermes) were said to have come to Lystra in disguise. No one gave them hospitality. Only two old peasants, Philemon and his wife, Baucis, took them in and were kind to them. In reprisal, the entire population was wiped out by the gods except Philemon and Baucis. These two were made guardians of a great temple and turned into giant trees when they died.

The people of Lystra were determined not to let such a thing happen again. The cripple's healing was so great a miracle that the natives were sure Barnabas and Paul were these two gods come back again. Barnabas was evidently a man of noble presence, so they took him for Zeus. Because Paul was the speaker, they thought him to be Hermes, and prepared to offer a sacrifice to their gods.

Discuss the following statements based on verses 14-17:

vv. 14-15a   People of faith do not want the worship of people.
             Agree _____ Disagree _____. Why? _____

vv. 15b-17   People of faith should be prepared to turn *every* situation into an occasion for a Christian witness.
             Agree _____ Disagree _____ Not sure _____

Dream the impossible. What are some miracles needed in your life?
             1. _____
             2. _____

Do you think Paul's recovery (vv. 19-20) was natural or a miracle? _____ Why? _____

Ponder this thought:

We should not presume on God, but people of faith should trust God so completely that they do not shrink from living dangerously if such is in their line of duty for Christ. Agree _____ Disagree _____

Read 14:21-25

What words describe the ministry of Paul and Barnabas in Lystra, Iconium, and Antioch (v. 22)? _____

Are there some personal implications in verse 22 for you in your situation:

In the home? Yes _____ No _____ What? _____
On the job? Yes _____ No _____ What? _____
In the neighborhood? Yes _____ No _____ What? _____

Does verse 23 suggest the importance of pastoral leadership for local churches? Yes _____ No _____ Not sure _____

From verses 21, 24-26 trace on the map, p. 12, the return journey from Derbe to Antioch in Syria. Let one person read the place names while each member traces the route on his own map.

In verse 26, what words describe the commission of Paul and Barnabas to their missionary task? _____

In verse 27, the two Christian workers could have focused on the negative and their rejection. Instead, the thrust of their report is upon the positive. They "reported all that God had done through them and how he had opened the door of faith to the Gentiles" (NIV).

What are you seeing in your own ministry? In the ministry of your local church? Is it the negative or the positive? How much does what you look for and find affect your effectiveness for Christ? Much _____ Some _____ Little _____

A Time for Reflection

What qualities of Christian service are reflected in the ministries of Paul and Barnabas?

v. 1   Love _____ Persuasion _____ Dominance _____
v. 3   Humility _____ Faith _____ Courage _____
vv. 7, 20   Perseverance _____ Encouragement _____ Fear _____
v. 9   Courage _____ Humility _____ Faith _____
vv. 14-15   Encouragement _____ Faith _____ Humility _____

v. 22   Persuasion _____ Faith _____ Encouragement _____
v. 27   Accountability _____ Courage _____ Aggressiveness _____
Which of these character qualities is most lacking in your life? _____

With which trait has God already given you some help? _____
Thank Him for it.

If time permits and the setting is appropriate, several members could share their concerns about weak character qualities in their lives and request prayer support from the group.

Prayer Time

Turn to "My Ministry of Intercessory Prayer" in the back of this book. This is your personal prayer list.

Spend a few minutes reflecting on the question, "What does the Lord want me to do as a result of this Bible study?" Identify specific people and concerns that you want to lift to the Father in prayer. Return to this list throughout the week.

What witnesses of love and care, what acts of encouragement, or what ministries of service does God want you to do or say? Be specific. Write down the who, where, and how. Share some of these items with others in the group before you pray together.

Conclude the session with prayer, focusing on the needs represented in the group.

Something to Think About or Do

Suggested verses to memorize: 2 Pet. 1:5-8. Study the character qualities listed in 2 Pet. 1:5-7, NIV. For each quality, write an "I will" statement identifying specifically something you will do this week to improve that particular quality in your life.

Regarding faith, I will _____.
Regarding goodness, I will _____.
Regarding knowledge, I will _____.
Regarding self-control, I will _____.
Regarding perseverance, I will _____.
Regarding godliness, I will _____.
Regarding brotherly kindness, I will _____.
Regarding love, I will _____.

Using your favorite translation, read Acts 15:1-41 for next week's study.

3   Resolving Conflicts in the Church

ACTS 15:1-35

Introduction

Chapter 15 records one of the most important decisions of the Early Church. The fact that Luke devotes a long chapter to this Jerusalem Council is proof that he considered the issue crucial.

The growth of the Jewish-Gentile church at Antioch and the success of Paul's first missionary journey in which he won so many Gentile converts precipitated this major problem.

All agreed that the Christian message centered around the experience of salvation. This they understood as deliverance from the guilt, power, and pollution of sin, issuing in a life of likeness to Christ. All agreed that salvation was obtained through faith in Christ. But Paul and Barnabas were preaching that it was by faith alone "without the deeds of the law" (cf. Rom. 3:19-31). On the other hand, certain members of the Jerusalem church insisted that salvation came through faith in Christ—plus circumcision and observance of the Mosaic Law.

Opening Prayer

Father, we approach this study with humility and fear—fear that the breadth and depth of Your truth will be limited by our narrow vision and shallow thinking.

Enlarge our understanding of the gospel. Enable us to discover the breadth of Your love within which differences between committed Christians can be resolved in growth-producing ways.

How much we want to learn from You today! Through Christ we pray. Amen.

Review

Spend a few minutes looking back over your week with the Lord.

Perhaps you could ask: What can I praise God for: Answers to prayer? Blessings? Miracles?

What do I need to confess to the Father and/or to others? Failure? Sin? Hurts? Needs?

What can I share with the group that will build them up in Jesus? Lessons learned? Insights gained?

Use the space below to record your experiences:

What the Lord Has Done	My Responses: Praise/Confession/Sharing

Scriptural Analysis and Application

Read chapter 15 with pen in hand, writing your observations in the space provided below.

Who were the persons involved? (vv. 1, 5, 7-11, 12, 13-20) _____

What was the issue discussed? _____

Where was the council held? _____

Why was the problem important? _____

How was the issue resolved? _____

Read the following explanation by Dr. Wm. Greathouse of the problems facing the Jerusalem Council:

1. Christian Pharisees in Jerusalem were reacting to a dual problem which arose as the gospel moved out of Judea:

   a. Simon Peter, the number one apostle, had baptized Cornelius and his household into the Church, in recognition of their baptism with the Spirit (just as the original 120 had been filled on the Day of Pentecost) (11:1-18).

   b. Paul and Barnabas had been receiving hundreds of uncircumcised Gentiles into the Church on the basis of faith in Christ, totally disregarding the law of Moses (11:19—14:27).

2. What Peter had done was accepted because of the evident marks of divine approval which accompanied his action at Joppa. But Paul and Barnabas had created a completely new situation. The Church was being flooded with Gentiles! Jewish Christians feared that this influx of new converts would undermine Christian moral standards.

3. The Christian Pharisees "stood up and said, 'They have to be circumcised and told to obey the Law of Moses'" (15:5, TEV). For these persons the Church of Jesus Christ was simply a new sect of Judaism. These Judaizers, who had simply added belief in Jesus' resurrection and messiahship to their prior belief in the doctrine of the Resurrection, remained legalists at heart. They insisted, "'You cannot be saved unless you are circumcised as the Law of Moses requires'" (15:1, TEV). Salvation was not by grace through faith for them, but by faith *plus* works.

Read 15:1-6

For the geographical setting of this problem, locate on a Bible map, Antioch, Phoenicia, Samaria, and Jerusalem. Antioch lay 300 miles north of Jerusalem, close to predominantly Gentile territory.

Luke says (v. 1) that the men came *down* from Judea to Antioch. We normally speak of going *down* south and *up* north. But to the Jews, going anywhere from Jerusalem was to go *down*.

Why do you think Paul and Barnabas were so firm in resisting the pro-Jewish teaching (v. 2)? _____

Who appointed Paul and Barnabas to undertake this assignment (vv. 2-3)? _____

What news made the Christians in Phoenicia and Samaria rejoice (v. 3)? _____

What did Paul and Barnabas report to the leaders of the Church in Jerusalem (v. 4)? _____

Who raised the issue about observing Jewish customs (v. 5)? _____

Explore with the group what modern-day counterparts of circumcision and the Law of Moses may exist among Christians. List ideas of your own below.

    1. _____
    2. _____

Read 15:6-11

Why do you think Peter would be the one to speak in favor of Gentile liberty (recall 10:23-29)? _____

Peter's testimony shows that the distinction between Jew and Gentile means nothing to God, who knows the human heart (vv. 8-9). Agree _____ Disagree _____

Salvation is not a matter of being circumcised but of having the heart cleansed by faith (v. 9). Agree _____ Disagree _____

Wherever the Spirit of God is at work quickening and sanctifying men and women, there the Church is (vv. 8-9). Agree _____ Disagree _____

Read 15:12-21

Who took the initiative in guiding the council to its decision (v. 13)?

What was the basic truth that guided the council's decision (v. 14)?

Ask a member to read aloud Amos 9:11-12, the scripture that James quoted as evidence for God's plan. What phrase in Amos 9:12 is parallel to "all the Gentiles" in Acts 15:17? _____

What five provisions were in James's solution (vv. 19-20)?

    v. 19 _____
    v. 20 _____
    v. 20 _____
    v. 20 _____
    v. 20 _____

What guidance do you think the Jerusalem church gives us when faced with the necessity of compromise in areas of Christian behavior? __

Rate yourself on the scale below: 1 is no problem, 7 is to reject the position as completely unchristian.

I have difficulty with Christians who are constant critics.	1 2 3 4 5 6 7
People should not buy on Sundays.	1 2 3 4 5 6 7
Christians should not go to the movies.	1 2 3 4 5 6 7
Saturday is the Lord's Day.	1 2 3 4 5 6 7
The Bible is without error in all it affirms.	1 2 3 4 5 6 7
Christians should not smoke cigarettes.	1 2 3 4 5 6 7
Christians should not be overweight.	1 2 3 4 5 6 7
It's OK to play Uno or Rook with your family.	1 2 3 4 5 6 7

What does this quiz tell you about your tolerance level? _____

Explore your position with others in the group. How wide is the opinion spread on each item? _____

Let's define legalism as making behavior the most important or a very important measure of Christlikeness. Are the following statements true or false?

_____ Legalism enforces tendencies toward self-righteousness.
_____ Legalism is easier to regulate than the freedom of grace.
_____ People are legalists because of their rigid personalities.
_____ Few people react negatively to legalism.

Why is tolerance necessary in the church? _____

At what point can tolerance no longer be accepted? _____

Read 15:22-35

Explore the ways in which the church reached its decision.

v. 22 _____
v. 23 _____

v. 24 _____
v. 28 _____
v. 29 _____

Concluding Thoughts

Could it be that God is more interested in our love for one another than in complete agreement on every detail? Yes _____ No _____ Not sure _____

The disagreements give opportunity to express love for one another. True _____ False _____

To be able to love and work with someone who doesn't completely agree with us is evidence of God's love at work in our lives. Yes _____ No _____

A Moment for Reflection

Briefly share one insight from the session which is significant to you. How do you plan to include it into your life-style this week?

Prayer Time

Turn to the section in the back of this study entitled "My Ministry of Intercessory Prayer."

Spend a few minutes reflecting upon the question, "What does the Lord want me to do as a result of this Bible study session?" Identify those for whom you need to pray. Return to this list throughout the week.

What witness of love and care does God want you to do or say? Be specific. Write down the who, where, and how.

Conclude the session with group prayer, focusing on the needs represented in your prayer lists.

Something to Think About or Do

Suggested verses to remember: Eph. 4:1-3.

Ponder the words of Paul in Eph. 4:25-32 regarding "speaking the truth in love" (v. 15). Paul here gives practical expression to how we can keep the unity of the Spirit through the bond of peace. Note the chart that follows.

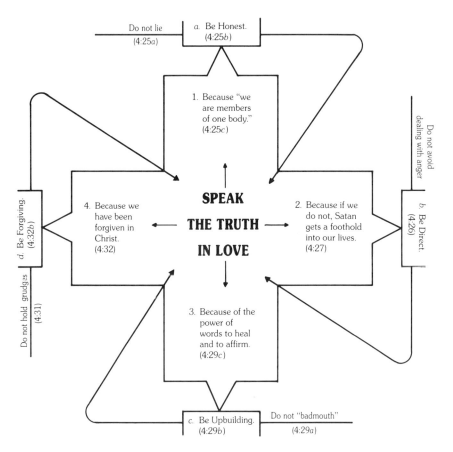

For next week read Acts 15:36—16:40.

4   Obeying the Will of the Lord

ACTS 15:36—16:40

Introduction

"The Church exists by mission as fire exists by burning" (Emil Brunner). The Church is mission. Through the Church, Christ is continuing His redemptive ministry among men.

The story of Acts 16 is a beautiful lesson in the providential guidance of God in the life of the Church as it lives under the direction of the Spirit of Jesus to accomplish His will.

This chapter continues the record, begun in 15:36, of Paul's second missionary journey. See the chart, p. 11. Paul proposed that he and Barnabas revisit and check on the progress of the new churches they had left behind them in Asia Minor.

We see here the hand of God guiding the Early Church westward toward Europe. There seems to be an urgency in the matter which leaves no doubt about the divine intention. In the days of the apostles He led the Church westward into Europe. Later from the European base the gospel radiated to the ends of the earth.

In these tasks, God used human agents to carry forward His program for the Church. He still uses us.

Opening Prayer

Father, we will use familiar words today. Not new and flashy terms, but words like "the will of God," "being saved," and "God's sovereignty." Pour new content into these old and familiar words.

In this multifaceted chapter, teach us something about yourself and about ourselves which we have not known before. In Jesus' name. Amen.

Review

Spend a few minutes in review. Look back over the past week with the Lord and reflect upon it. Perhaps you could ask:

What can I praise God for? Answers to prayer? Blessings? Miracles of
forgiveness?

What do I need to confess? Failure? Hurts? An unforgiving spirit?

What can I share with the group that will build them up in Jesus?
Truth? Light? Help in forgiving one who has wronged me?

Use the space provided below to write out your responses.

What the Lord Has Done	My Responses: Praise/Confession/Sharing

Scriptural Analysis and Application

As you read through the scripture for an overview, record answers to
the questions below.

Who are the key persons in this account? _____

Locate on your map, p. 12, all the places that Paul visited.

Why was the party making this trip (15:36)? _____

How did Paul and his party travel?

       1. _____

       2. _____

Read 15:36-41

What did Paul and Barnabas agree on (v. 36)? _____

On what did they disagree (vv. 37-38)? _____

Let a member be prepared to read aloud to the group these comments by Dr. Greathouse:

> It is heartening to discover that God has always used men
> who are fully human. Paul and Barnabas were Spirit-filled men,

but they had the treasure of the gospel in human vessels (2 Cor. 4:7). Their very strengths turned out to be their weakness. Paul was a man of intense dedication who demanded of his co-workers the same flinchless discipleship. John Mark had failed him at a crucial moment on the first journey. It was unthinkable that they should take him with them again, Paul reasoned.

But Barnabas, whose very name meant "Son of Encouragement," felt the young man should be given a second chance. Besides, Mark was his cousin! Barnabas' determination to take Mark led to sharp differences between two men who had long been associated in the work of the gospel. It must have been a sad and painful moment when Barnabas took Mark and set out for Cyprus. It may have been the last time these old friends ever saw each other.

What shall we make of this? Simply that strong men have strong convictions which at times lead to clashes. We are hardly in a position to judge whether Paul or Barnabas, or both, showed an unchristlike spirit. . . . At any rate, the difference led to no final breach. Paul's subsequent references to Barnabas are kind and complimentary (1 Cor. 9:6; Col. 4:10). And John Mark regained Paul's confidence. Paul recommended him to the Colossian church (Col. 4:10), and spoke of him as one of "my fellowlabourers" (Philem. 24). Shortly before his martyrdom, Paul wrote Timothy: "Take Mark, and bring him with thee; for he is profitable to me for the ministry" (2 Tim. 4:11).

Do sanctified people ever disagree? Yes _____ No _____. Do they hold grudges? Yes _____ No _____. Are they willing to admit they are wrong? Yes _____ No _____.

Read 16:1-10

Study these observations by Dr. Greathouse.

Three times in these 10 verses the guidance of the Spirit is indicated.

What guidance is given in:
v. 6 _____
v. 7 _____
vv. 9-10 _____

The first two instances offer us no clue as to the nature of the Spirit's guidance. Some believe the Spirit spoke within the consciousness of the apostle, others that He spoke through a prophet. The question of divine guidance is complex. Exercising reverent care, let us attempt to erect a framework for our thought. (1) God has a plan—big enough to encompass the world and particular enough to include you and me. (2) A part of God's overall strategy was the creation of free beings. We are not pawns in the hands of Deity. God delights in our responsible choices, just as an earthly parent thrills in the wise choices of his son. In a great many areas of our lives God's will is that we make intelligent, Christlike choices.

How can you apply the last statement in your own life? _____

This leads to a further point. (3) Consecration introduces us into the large room of that "good, and acceptable, and perfect will of God" (Rom. 12:1-2). In many small choices that knowledge is right at hand. When we are about to make a wrong moral choice, the Spirit immediately checks us (Rom. 8:14). In the more weighty decisions of life a devoted Christian will give himself to a thoughtful, prayerful *seeking* of God's will. He will pray until he has "prayed through"—through the maze of human desires and feelings until their clamor has subsided. In the hush that follows, a voice may usually be heard, saying, "This is the way, walk ye in it."

Have you had such experiences? Yes ____ No ____

Candor forces us to admit that it is sometimes difficult to tune in on that Voice. Then it is well to seek the counsel of spiritual friends, for often the Spirit speaks to us through others. In regard to visions and impressions (4) we must always heed the admonition to "test the spirits" (1 John 4:1, NASB). God never leads us contrary to the written Word or to the Spirit of Christ. And when a vision is from the Lord, the door is always open. God never leads us into a blind alley.

If you or someone you know has apparently been mistaken about "the Lord's will," share the experience with the group.

Finally, (5) we may be absolutely confident that, if the issue is really critical for God's purposes, He will unfailingly make His mind known. If after we have done all we know to discern His will we are still in doubt, we may assume God is willing to *trust our sanctified judgment.*

A recap of Dr. Greathouse's five guidelines to finding God's will follows. Which points are you familiar with? Which are new?

USED NEW

____ ____   Acknowledge your place in God's plan
____ ____   Make intelligent, Christlike choices
____ ____   Pray through on weighty decisions
____ ____   Test the spirits and seek others' counsel
____ ____   When in doubt, use sanctified judgment

"God's will for our character is primarily revealed in Christ . . . while His will for our career and the related details of our lives must be sought by each of us for himself." Agree ____ Disagree ____ Why or why not? ____

Garry Friesen, in his book *Decision Making and the Will of God,* [1] discusses four principles which he calls the "way of wisdom." Check the one that you find most difficult to incorporate into your Christian decision making.

1. In those areas specifically addressed by the Bible, the revealed commands and principles of God (His moral will) are to be obeyed. ____

2. In those areas where the Bible gives no command or principle (nonmoral decisions) the believer is free and responsible to choose his own course of action. Any decision made within the moral will of God is acceptable to God. ____

3. In these nonmoral decisions, the objective of the Christian is to make wise choices on the basis of spiritual expediency. ____

4. In all decisions, the believers should humbly submit, in advance, to the outworking of God's sovereign will as it touches the decision. ____

Read 16:11-15

Dr. Greathouse has additional words regarding "Divine Purpose":

The Spirit's hastening Paul on to Troas and thence to Macedonia was but the outworking of a divine purpose which to us is of great moment. The evangelizing of Europe was implicit in that move.

Paul had no way of knowing the full import of that mission. The instant his foot touched European soil, a chain reaction was set off that changed the course of Western civilization and that, after two thousand years, has touched your life and mine with transforming power.

According to the above comments, who was responsible for our receiving the gospel in Western countries? _____ Was he aware of the immense outreach his trip to Macedonia would trigger? _____ In light of this, how important is your small witness and mine? _____

Dr. Greathouse continues:

God's purposes are not always immediately apparent. Things often just seem to happen, with no point whatever. But we must not judge on the basis of the seeming. We need the long view to grasp God's strategy. The plot of a story is not usually seen except in retrospect. . . .

Someday all of us will be able to look back—if we love God—and perceive the purpose in the hitherto jumble and tangle of events . . . If we live Spirit-guided lives—seeking first, last, and only the will of God—God will gather up every sorrow or tragedy and . . . weave a design that one day we shall rejoice to see.

Do you agree with these comments? Yes ___ No ___ Why or why not? _____

Notice in verse 6 Luke refers to "Paul and his companions," and in verse 10 he writes, "We got ready at once to leave for Macedonia" (both NIV). Throughout the rest of the book the "we" passages alert us that Luke was with the party. He first joined them at Troas.

Why did Paul and Silas go to the riverside on the Sabbath (v. 13)?

Apparently there were only a few Jews in Philippi. If there were as many as 10 heads of families in a community, they were expected to provide a synagogue. If there were too few to maintain a formal place of worship, they often met out of doors.

In your own words write what you think happened to Lydia where Luke says: "The Lord opened her heart to respond to Paul's message" (NIV). _____

Read 16:16-34

What do you think troubled Paul about the behavior of this slave girl (vv. 16-19)?

___ She was giving them unfavorable publicity.
___ Her owners were exploiting her.
___ She was not telling the truth.

The slave owners charged Paul and Silas with anti-Roman teaching (v. 21). What was their real reason for having the missionaries arrested? ___

Ask one member to read aloud verses 23-30.

If Paul and Silas were familiar with your songbook, what hymn do you think they would have sung in the Philippian jail? _____

Why do you think the jailer planned to kill himself (v. 27)? _____

How could the heathen jailer have known enough about salvation to ask, "What must I do to be saved?" (v. 30)? (See v. 17.) _____

Who besides the jailer were converted that night (vv. 31-34)? _____

A Christian father is usually a strong influence for Christ in his own family. Why do you think this is so? _____

Read 16:35-40
Why do you think Paul demanded that the Roman magistrates come personally to release him and Silas (v. 37)?
_____ Favorable publicity for Christ
_____ To humble the officials
_____ To make the officials more careful next time
_____ Other reason? Explain. _____
What fact frightened the magistrates (v. 38)? _____

What words in verse 40 indicate that Paul and Silas left a Christian congregation in Philippi? _____
What do you think it means to believe on the Lord Jesus Christ? Write the answer in your own words: _____

Share your answer with the group.

Prayer Time
Turn to the section entitled "My Ministry of Intercessory Prayer." Is there someone comparable to the slave girl whom you could help? Is there anyone like the jailer and his family in your neighborhood? Return to your prayer list throughout the week.
Share some of these items with others in the group before you pray together.
Conclude the session with prayer for unsaved persons known to members of the group.

Something to Think About or Do

Suggested verse to remember: Acts 16:31

During the week prepare a character study of Lydia. Recall God's work in her life. Who among your acquaintances most nearly resembles Lydia? Plan to express to her your appreciation for her Christian faith and life.

Before next week, read Acts 17:1-35.

5 Successfully Communicating the Gospel

ACTS 17:1-34

Introduction

This week's passage shows the varied responses evoked by the gospel. In Thessalonica, Paul and his party faced ridicule and hostility. In Berea they found a responsive group ready to test their message by the Scriptures. In Athens, there were self-sufficient skeptics who scoffed at Paul's gospel.

How typical are these responses in our own experiences as we seek to be witnesses for Christ?

Opening Prayer

Father, we want so much to share what Christ has done for us. Yet we are too often paralyzed by fear—fear of rejection, fear of inadequate Bible knowledge, fear of unanswerable questions, and of failure.

Use our study this week to counter the fear and thwart the dread. Teach us to move out where the people are, to share confidently the Good News. May we learn from Your Word various approaches to different situations. We really want to obey our Lord's command, "You will be my witnesses."

Teach us today. In our Savior's name. Amen.

Review

Spend a few minutes in review. Use the space provided below to write your responses. Look back over the past week with the Lord and reflect upon it. Perhaps you could ask, What opportunities have I had to witness for Christ? How well have I used them? Are there places where I have failed to use the opportunity?

Opportunities the Lord Has Given	My Responses: Praise/Confession/Sharing

Scriptural Analysis and Application

Read the entire chapter for a survey of the contents. Write the background data in the space provided below.

Who were the members of Paul's party? _____

In what places did they preach? _____

Where did the people test Paul's message by the Scriptures? _____

_____

When did Paul go to Athens? _____

How did the people of Athens respond to the message of the Resurrection? _____

Read 17:1-9

What is implied in the words of verses 2-3, "he reasoned with them from the Scriptures, explaining and proving that the Christ had to suffer and rise from the dead" (NIV)? In your own words describe what you think you would have seen Paul doing if he had visited your church. _____

What words show us Paul's methods?

v. 2 _____

v. 2 _____

v. 3 _____

In Thessalonica and in Berea, Paul's ministry was confined largely to the Jews and Jewish proselytes. How did this influence his method of witnessing (vv. 2-3, 11)? _____

What words describe Paul's message (v. 3)? _____

What forms of opposition developed in Thessalonica?

v. 5 _____

v. 5 _____

v. 5 _____

v. 6 _____

We do not know much about Jason, Paul's host in Thessalonica. Let someone read aloud Rom. 16:21. Here Jason was one of Paul's companions who sent greetings to Rome. "He is probably the same person. Paul calls him a kinsman (KJV), which means a Jew" (ISBE).

Read 17:10-15

What is implied in the phrase "for they received the message with great eagerness and examined the Scriptures every day to see if what Paul said was true" (v. 11, NIV)?

YES   NO

_____ _____ Interest

_____ _____ Devotion

_____ _____ Worldly concerns

_____ _____ Spiritual hunger

What is needed on our part today if we are to be characterized by the response of the Bereans?

1. _____

2. _____

What was Paul's chief strategy when one group rejected his message (vv. 10, 14-15)? _____

Why do you think Paul left Silas and Timothy in Berea (v. 14)? ____

Read 17:16-34

In Athens, Paul ministered in the synagogue, but also in the marketplace (v. 17). The larger part of the chapter is given over to his address to the Greek philosophers (of the Areopagus, v. 19) on Mars Hill. Under these conditions, why would Paul not quote from the Old Testament as he had done in Thessalonica and Berea? _____

Why would he, instead, quote from Greek writers (v. 28)? _____

Was Paul structuring his approach to the ability of his audience to understand? Yes _____ No _____ Not sure _____

Thinking About Paul's Sermon

What do you think Paul was trying to accomplish with his audience? (See the introduction, verses 22-23.) _____

What does Paul assert about the nature of God (vv. 24-25)? _____

What does he assert about the nature of man (v. 26)?
1. _____
2. _____

Why did God create man (v. 27)? _____

What does Paul assert about man's religious nature (v. 28)? _____

Why does Paul argue that we should reject idolatry (v. 29)? _____

Why was God more lenient toward the sin of idolatry in earlier times (v. 30)? _____

What do you think Paul means when he says God comands all men to repent (v. 30)? In your own words define repentance. _____

Who do you think is "the man" God has appointed to judge the world (v. 31, NIV)? _____ Why is that Man qualified to judge the world with justice?

What was the truth of the Christian message that offended the heathen philosophers (v. 32)? _____

The word "successful" is used in the title of this lesson. Did Paul fail at Athens? Yes _____ No _____ Not sure _____. Most scholars think not (v. 34). Read aloud in the group 1 Cor. 4:2. God measures our success by our faithfulness, not by the number of converts who are won.

A Pause for Reflection

In this chapter, what were the various responses to the gospel?
v. 4 _____
v. 5 _____
vv. 11-12 _____

v. 18 _____
v. 20 _____
v. 32a _____
v. 32b _____
v. 34 _____

Consider These Thoughts

For Paul, Christian faith means complete surrender to Christ. Faith is not merely intellectual assent to the truth of the gospel. Faith is the act of the whole man—the persuasion of the mind that God loves me, and through the sacrifice of Calvary, He is willing to save me. But faith also includes obedience of the will. Faith says, "I surrender all: all my sins, all my self-righteousness, all my efforts to save myself."

Faith is a dynamic fusion of surrender, obedience, and trust which includes repentance. Repentance is an about-face, a turning from sin to God. It is not giving up this little thing or that. Repentance is changing your whole thought and feeling about God, Christ, sin, and yourself. It is an absolute and unconditional surrender of your heart and life to God.

Prayer Time

Turn to the section in the back of this study guide entitled "My Ministry of Intercessory Prayer." Spend a few minutes reflecting on the questions: How have three or four members of my family or friends responded to the gospel? Are there some of them whose faith I can encourage? Are there some who have not yet repented? If so, what does Christ want me to do about it?

Conclude the session with a prayer that God will help all of us to be faithful witnesses for Christ to those who know us but do not know Him.

Something to Think About or Do

Suggested passage to memorize: 2 Cor. 5:17-20

Before next week, read Acts 18:1-28.

6 The Community of Faith Ministering

ACTS 18:1-28

Introduction

Acts 18 is a chapter on ministry—not only the work of Paul, the preacher, but of Apollos, the teacher; and of Aquila and Priscilla, the encouragers.

All of God's people are called to ministry—the continuing work of Jesus in the world; each one using the gifts given to him by the Holy Spirit. Ministry is a function of the whole church. It is not something to which only a few persons are called, trained, and ordained. Rather, all Christians are ministers; all of us are called to represent Christ in our circles of influence—wherever they may be.

Opening Prayer

Father, if the Church is to be renewed, we believe it will happen when all of us respond to Your call and find ways to represent You in the home, in our community, on the job, and in the church.

Father, only You can break through and correct our vision. Show us human need and show us our opportunities. Enlarge our vision to see that to which we have been called—all of us—as Your children. We pray through Christ. Amen.

Review

Spend a few minutes in review. Look back over your past week with the Lord and reflect upon it.

What can I praise God for? Answers to prayer? Peace even under stress? Miracles? Opportunities for ministry?

What do I need to confess to the Father or to others? Failure? Hurts? Frustrations or feelings of ineffectiveness?

What can I share with the group that will build them up in Jesus? A testimony? A new insight?

Use the space provided below to write out your responses.

What the Lord Has Done	My Responses: Praise/Confession/Sharing

Scriptural Analysis and Application

As you survey chapter 18, look for answers to the five questions below.

Who are the new people we have not met before? _____

What promise did the Lord give to Paul? _____

Where is Corinth in relation to Athens (see map)? _____

When did Apollos come to Ephesus? _____

How long did Paul remain in Corinth? _____

Preaching (Read 18:1-11)

This chapter continues the story of Paul's second missionary journey (see chart, p. 11). The story began at 15:36.

With whom did Paul make his home in Corinth? (Acts 18:3) _____ _____ Why? _____

Ask a member to read aloud 1 Cor. 2:1-5.

How did Paul describe his own attitude as he began his ministry at Corinth (1 Cor. 2:3)? _____

Write here the focus he adopted for his preaching at Corinth (1 Cor. 2:2). _____

In verse 5, why do you think Paul was able to give full time to his preaching after Silas and Timothy came to Corinth? _____

What had Paul been doing on weekdays before Silas and Timothy arrived (v. 3)? _____

Study the following article by Dr. William Greathouse on the subject of preaching.

Let us think of Paul in the role of preaching. In the New Testament sense preaching is the *proclamation* of good news. To preach is to herald glad tidings. To preach is to announce that "God hath visited and redeemed his people" in His Son, Jesus Christ. It is to call men to repent and believe the gospel and to experience the gift of the Holy Spirit.

The great and good news of the New Testament is that God has brought to pass all that is foretold in the prophets—the kingdom of God is here! The Messiah is no longer a hope; He has come—and His name is Jesus. Preaching is setting forth the life, death, resurrection, ascension, and coming again of Jesus—in such a way as men are made to see that they must repent and be saved. A study of the sermons in Acts shows that at the heart of preaching is the story of the Cross as both the deed of wicked men as well as the deed of God for man's salvation—but never the Cross as an end.

The Jesus whom men put to death, GOD has raised and made Lord and Christ! He has exalted this Jesus to His own right hand where He sheds forth the Holy Spirit in baptismal fullness! Preachers of the gospel not only call men to repent of their sins; they also ask, "Have you received the Holy Spirit since you believed?" Preaching is doing the work of an evangelist.

To those who are perishing preaching is sheer nonsense, but to those of us who are being saved, it is the wisdom of God and the power of God (see 1 Cor. 1:17-31). By the foolishness of preaching (not foolish preaching!) God saves those who believe. The importance of preaching is underscored also in Rom. 10:9-17. "For whosoever shall call upon the name of the Lord shall be saved. How then shall they call on him in whom they have not believed? and how shall they believe in him of whom they have not heard? *and how shall they hear without a preacher?*" New Testament salvation is the gift of God to those who believe the good news of Christ.

God *called* Paul to this task (Gal. 1:15-16). He still calls preachers to this ministry. Although in a sense every believer is a preacher, we recognize that God lays His hands upon certain persons whom He thrusts out into a full-time public ministry of the Word. Without such preachers the Church could not exist. The responsibility of the Church is to *send* preachers. "And how shall they preach, except they be sent? as it is written, How beautiful are the feet of them that preach the gospel of peace, and bring glad tidings of good things!" (Rom. 10:15).

Lay Helpers (Read 18:12-23)

Divide into two small groups. Ask the first to list and briefly identify all the people named in Acts 18. Let them decide who, besides Aquila and Priscilla, helped Paul—and how they helped him.

Ask the second group to list four ways that Aquila and Priscilla helped Paul (vv. 1-3, 18-19, 24-26, 27).

If your group is small, you may want to pursue both tasks all together.

After both small groups have had sufficient time to complete their research, reassemble. As group No. 1 reports, discuss the ways different persons helped Paul. List similar ministries possible in our Christian life and service today.

    1. _____

    2. _____

    3. _____

As group No. 2 reports, discuss additional contemporary ways lay-persons in the congregation can help the preacher.

Verse 12 helps us date Paul's time in Corinth. An inscription at Delphi, dated A.D. 52, refers to "Gallio . . . proconsul of Achaia." Paul probably labored in Corinth about 51-52.

Teaching (Read 18:24-28)

Do you think Apollos might be considered the teacher of the group? Yes _____ No _____

If yes, what terms would lead you to think so?

    v. 24 _____

    v. 24 _____

    v. 25 _____

    v. 25 _____

Teaching is concerned with relating the Bible to matters of daily Christian living. Christian education takes place at the intersection of one's persistent life concerns and the gospel. Jesus was both Preacher and Teacher.

In the Scriptures, we frequently read, "He opened his mouth, and taught them."

Paul was one of the great teachers at Antioch (Acts 11:26). His letters are balanced between proclamation and teaching.

Some persons are more gifted than others in teaching, but by faithful study of the Bible we may improve our teaching ability and thereby minister to the Body of Christ and build it up in faith, love, and obedience.

Can you recall some teacher in the church who influenced your life for good? If so, be prepared to share your experience with the group.

What verse in this section shows the end of Paul's second missionary journey? _____

What verse indicates the beginning of his third journey? _____

Encouragers (Read again vv. 18-26)

Why are Aquila and Priscilla called "encouragers"? _____
_____

What was the deficiency in Apollos' preaching? _____
_____

What was the response of Aquila and Priscilla?
a. They started a whispering campaign and criticized Apollos. Yes ____ No ____
b. They initiated a movement to get him out of town. Yes ____ No ____
c. Write here from verse 26 what they did. _____
_____

Someone has said, "We may not be able to pray like Paul, preach like Peter, or teach like Apollos, but we can tell the love of Jesus as did Aquila and Priscilla."

Finding Our Gifts

Although we are called as Spirit-filled Christians to preach, teach and encourage, God also has other gifts. He gives each of us unique abilities to be used within the Body of Christ for its growth and edification. Preaching, teaching, and encouraging are three of the spiritual gifts mentioned in the Bible. Others are given in 1 Corinthians 12; Romans 12; Ephesians 4; and 1 Peter 5.

The following steps from Dr. James Garlow may help us identify our spiritual gift(s) for ministry within the community of faith.[1]

All members should be given sufficient time to answer each question. If time permits, share the conclusion.

Do you really want to know what gifts the Holy Spirit has given you so you can put them to work? _____

What are your goals for service? What gifts would it take to achieve these goals?

GOALS	GIFTS NEEDED
_____	_____
_____	_____
_____	_____

What are the greatest needs you see in your local congregation? What gifts would it take to minister to those needs?

CONGREGATIONAL NEEDS	GIFTS NEEDED
_____	_____
_____	_____
_____	_____

What are some ways you have served in the past? In those ministries, where were you most effective? What gifts were you using?

EFFECTIVE PAST MINISTRIES	GIFTS USED
_____	_____
_____	_____
_____	_____

Has the Holy Spirit confirmed any certain gift in your life? If so, what?
_____

Have other Christians affirmed certain gifts in you? If so, what? ____
_____

Prayer Time

Turn to the section in the back of this study, entitled "My Ministry of Intercessory Prayer." Are there one or more members of the group in whom you see gifts for ministry? If so, add their names to your prayer list. (1) Pray that God will encourage them to use those gifts. (2) Express your appreciation to them for their gifts.

Conclude the session with group prayer, focusing on needs around you and on the potential God has given each of you to minister helpfully to those needy persons.

Something to Think About or Do

Suggested passage to remember: Acts 18:9-10

Using your favorite translation, read Acts 19:1—20:38.

In order to cover both of these long chapters within the allotted time, ask three members to study the following passages carefully, and be prepared to tell the story to the group:

Acts 19:11-16
Acts 19:23-41
Acts 20:7-12

7   Our Ministry and Our Motives

ACTS 19:1—20:38

Introduction

Chapters 19—20 relate most of Paul's third missionary journey. The story begins at 18:23 and closes at 21:3. See the chart of these missionary journeys, p. 11. Paul had earlier tried to preach at Ephesus in the province of Asia near the beginning of his second journey (cf. 16:6), but at that time, God wanted him to work in Macedonia. Near the end of that journey, as we learned last week, Paul visited Ephesus briefly, leaving Aquila and Priscilla there to await his return from Jerusalem.

Ephesus was the capital of the province of Asia, known today as western Turkey; it included also the New Testament cities of Colosse, Laodicea, Philadelphia, Smyrna, and Sardis (see map in this study guide). During his three years in the province, Paul enjoyed a fruitful ministry. Luke reports: "All they which dwelt in Asia heard the word of the Lord Jesus, both Jews and Greeks" (19:10).

On this third missionary journey, following his ministry in Ephesus, Paul revisited cities in Macedonia and Greece. When he prepared to leave Corinth, he received word of a plot against his life. To avoid this plot, he changed his travel plans from Corinth and went back through Macedonia.

While all follow and mark Paul's journey on the map (p. 12), ask one member to trace the route, pointing out the places visited in these chapters.

Ephesus, 19:1-41	2½ years
Macedonia, 20:1-2	Brief stops at churches established on the second journey
Greece (Corinth), vv. 2-3	Three months
Berea, v. 4	Probable stops in Macedonia on the
Thessalonica, v. 4	return trip
Philippi, v. 6	
Troas, v. 6	Seven days
Assos, v. 13	

Mitylene, v. 14
Chios, v. 15
Samos, v. 15
Miletus, v. 15
Ephesus, v. 17
Coos, Rhodes, Patara, Cyprus,
Tyre, Ptolemais, 21:1-7
Caesarea, 21:8   End of the third journey

On this trip back to Jerusalem Paul met with the elders of the church of Ephesus (20:16-38). In speaking to them and reviewing his ministry among them, he reveals firsthand information as to his motives, message, and methods.

Opening Prayer

Father, we desire to drink deeply from the wellspring of Paul's life, character, goals, values, commitments, and priorities.

Use this session as we study another episode in the unfolding story of a great Christian and great leader. May our lives reflect the Christian growth that You desire for us. In Jesus' name. Amen.

Review

Spend a few minutes in review. Look back over the past week with the Lord and reflect upon it. Perhaps you could ask:

What can I praise God for? Answers to prayer? An opportunity for ministry? A personal experience of salvation?

What do I need to confess to the Father or to others? Failure? Hurts? Sins? Needs?

What truth or testimony can I share with the group that will build them up in Jesus?

Use the space provided below to write out your responses.

What the Lord Has Done	My Responses: Praise/Confession/Sharing

Scriptural Analysis and Application

Read 19:1-10

Paul's ministry has been termed a "calling" ministry. To what did he call the Ephesian Christians (Acts 20:20-21)?

1. _____

2. _____

In addition to the call to repentance and faith, reflect on the thoughts by Dr. Wm. Greathouse as he explains this passage.

> In beginning his ministry in Asia Minor, Paul began with the small group of "disciples" which made up the local church in Ephesus. He discovered that they were but imperfect Christians. They had little life or power. He put a question to them which is absolutely basic: "Did you receive the Holy Spirit when you became believers?" (NEB). The query stymied them. "We have not even heard the Holy Spirit has been given" (NASB margin). This can only mean these disciples *had not heard of Pentecost.*
>
> The Ephesian disciples had been taught accurately "the things concerning Jesus," but they "knew only the baptism of John"—the baptism of repentance and faith in the coming Christ. They apparently knew only the events of Jesus' earthly ministry, but had not heard of Calvary, Easter, or Pentecost. So Paul completed their knowledge of Christ, gave them Christian baptism as promissory of the baptism with the Spirit, laid his hands upon them, and brought them into the Pentecostal fullness of the Spirit.
>
> Scholars refer to this event as "the Ephesian Pentecost."

Four such historic outpourings of the Spirit are recorded in Acts. Ask three members to read aloud for the group the following passages:

1. The Jerusalem Pentecost—2:1-4
2. The Samaritan Pentecost—8:14-17
3. The Roman Pentecost—10:44-46

Each represents the breakthrough of the gospel into a new culture and the incorporation of a new group of believers into the Spirit-filled Body of Christ.

Conclusion: Only a Spirit-filled church can become God's instrument for bringing His kingdom into the affairs of men. The first and foremost question for any church is still: "Did you receive the Holy Spirit when you became believers?" Do you know the person and power of the indwelling Holy Spirit? Are you filled with the Holy Spirit? Are you experiencing that flowing of the Spirit through you which Jesus promised? (See John 7:37-39.)

Dwight L. Moody confessed, "For the first seven years of my Christian life I was as ignorant of the Holy Spirit as the disciples at Ephesus." What about you? What about your church? Until a body of Christians know the reality and power of being filled with the Spirit, they are not ready to do anything significant for God.

If God has filled you with the Holy Spirit, be prepared to share your testimony with the group.

Verse 9 refers to Christianity as "the way." (See also 9:2; 19:23; 22:4; 24:14, 22.) This popular name for the Christian movement shows us that Christianity does not simply mean believing certain things; it means living in a certain manner, putting these beliefs into practice. Christianity is not just a system of belief; it is a way of life.

How much does Christianity, as a way of life, run counter to the way of the world? Completely _____ Much _____ Little _____

Let the person assigned tell the story of 19:11-16. Then to see the results of God's power working in Ephesus, read aloud 19:17-20.

Read 19:21-41

Paul's ministry has been described as "confrontational" as well as a "calling" ministry.

Ask the assigned member to tell the story of 19:23-41.

Why was Paul's preaching a threat to the silversmiths? _____

What aspects of our culture do you think should be challenged by the gospel of Christ?

        1. _____

        2. _____

Can we be true followers of Christ and never confront our culture with His radical demands? Yes _____ No _____

Rank the following moral imperatives in order of need among your friends. Count 1 as most important; 4 as least important. If more than one imperative is absolutely necessary, you may rank more than one as a No. 1.

_____ Live in conscious relationship with God.

_____ Live in peace with your neighbor.

_____ Live as ministers of Christ.

_____ Live a life of holiness expressed in personal purity.

Discuss with the group your ranking and why you ranked them as you did.

Read 20:1-12

Retrace briefly on the map Paul's travels from Ephesus (v. 1) to Greece (Corinth, v. 2) and back to Troas (v. 6).

Ask the member assigned to tell to the group the story of verses 7-12.

Paul's ministry has been described as calling and confronting. It was also a caring ministry. What evidence is there to indicate the warm, personal dimensions of Paul?

v. 7 _____

v. 10 _____

v. 11 _____

Read 20:13-38

Why did Paul decide not to stop at Ephesus (v. 16)? _____

Who do you think would be included in the elders of the church at Ephesus (v. 17)? _____

How would you describe Paul's ministry in Ephesus?

v. 19 _____

v. 19 _____

v. 20 _____

v. 20 _____

v. 21 _____

v. 21 _____

v. 21 _____

Who was urging Paul to go to Jerusalem (v. 22)? _____

Has the Holy Spirit ever led you into some difficult task where you could not foresee the outcome (vv. 22-23)? Yes _____ No _____

If yes, be prepared to share your experience with the group.

Read together one man's commitment to God's purpose for his life:
"I consider my life worth nothing to me, if only I may finish the race and complete the task the Lord Jesus has given me—the task of testifying to the gospel of God's grace" (Acts 20:24, NIV).

Why could Paul leave the Ephesian congregation with a clear conscience about his ministry among them (vv. 26-27)? _____

What three responsibilities did Paul place upon the spiritual leaders of the church at Ephesus?

v. 28 _____

v. 28 _____

v. 28 _____

What danger did Paul warn them against (v. 30)? _____

Read together the selfless commitment of a Christlike pastor for his people:

> "Now I commit you to God and to the word of his grace, which can build you up and give you an inheritance among all those who are sanctified. I have not coveted anyone's silver or gold or clothing. You yourselves know that these hands of mine have supplied my own needs and the needs of my companions. In everything I did, I showed you that by this kind of hard work we must help the weak, remembering the words the Lord Jesus himself said: 'It is more blessed to give than to receive'" *(Acts 20:32-35, NIV).*

Prayer Time

Spend a few minutes reflecting on the question, "What unselfish ministries have I observed in the life of a Christian pastor?" Be prepared to share your experience with the group.

What witness of love and care or what acts of love and encouragement could you do for your pastor and family to express your love for them?

Conclude the session with prayers for each pastor who serves any member of the group.

Something to Think About or Do

Suggested verse to memorize: Acts 20:24

For the next session read Acts 21:1—22:29.

Assign two members to study carefully the following passages and be prepared to tell the stories to the group:

Acts 21:27-40

Acts 22:22-29

8   On to Jerusalem

ACTS 21:1—22:29

Introduction

Paul was deeply concerned for the unity of the Body of Christ. Later, from prison in Rome, he would write in the Ephesian letter:

> I urge you to live a life worthy of the calling you have received. Be completely humble and gentle; be patient, bearing with one another in love. Make every effort to keep the unity of the Spirit through the bond of peace *(4:1-3, NIV)*.

It was his concern for that unity that compelled him to return to Jerusalem with the offering which he had raised among the Gentile churches for suffering Jewish Christians. Let a member read those plans aloud to the group (1 Cor. 16:1-4).

In city after city Paul had received this offering from his Gentile churches to deliver to the Jerusalem Christians. The offering represented more than concern for the poor saints at Jerusalem; it was Paul's concern to bind these diverse elements together, thus sealing the oneness of the Church of Jesus Christ. It was imperative, therefore, that Paul, as the Apostle to the Gentiles, be there for the official presentation.

Opening Prayer

Lord, we are reminded again of the great convictions out of which Paul lived his Christian life. We are humbled. So many of our decisions are self-serving. His were so self-giving.

Work in us some transformation today. We desire deeply to be filled with Your Spirit that we see in the spirit of Paul. Make us bigger than we have been. Discipline us in our smallness. With Thomas Chisholm we pray,

Oh, to be like Thee! lowly in spirit,
  Holy and harmless, patient and brave;
Meekly enduring cruel reproaches,
  Willing to suffer others to save.

                                                    Amen.

Review

Spend a few minutes in review. Look back over the past week with the Lord and reflect upon it. Perhaps you could ask:

What can I praise God for? Some leadership of His Spirit? Some courage to press on? Some support of Christian friends?

What do I need to confess? Some fear in the face of opposition? Failure to follow the Spirit's promptings?

What can I share with the group that will build them up in Jesus?

Use the space provided below to write out your response.

What the Lord Has Done	My Responses: Praise/Confession/Sharing

Scriptural Analysis and Application

Read 21:1-14

What is implied in these verses regarding the attitude of the churches at Tyre and Caesarea for Paul (vv. 3-8)?

Concern for Paul's life: Yes _____ No _____

Love for the missionary: Yes _____ No _____

In verse 8, what is the meaning of the words describing Philip as "one of the Seven" (NIV)? (Read aloud in the group Acts 6:1-6.) _____

To sense Paul's complete devotion to God's work, read aloud in unison these verses:

"I am ready not only to be bound, but also to die in Jerusalem for the name of the Lord Jesus" *(21:13, NIV).*

"Christ will be exalted in my body, whether by life or by death. For to me, to live is Christ and to die is gain" *(Phil. 1:20-21, NIV).*

Read 21:15-26

What was the first concern of Paul and his group upon their arrival in Jerusalem (vv. 18-19)? _____

Why do you think this was important? _____

Read aloud the following explanation by Dr. Greathouse.

Upon his arrival in Jerusalem, Paul was warmly received by James and the other Jewish brethren. But Paul learned that the Jerusalem Christians were quite disturbed by a report that he was teaching "all the Jews which are among the Gentiles to forsake Moses, saying that they ought not to circumcise their children, neither to walk after the customs" (21:21). In order to allay the fears of the Jewish Christians, James suggested that Paul associate himself with four men who were under a vow and were about to go to the Temple for purification. Paul agreed to the proposal, apparently without any reluctance.

Paul's compliance with James' request clearly proves that he never regarded it as part of his work to dissuade born-again Jews from living as Jews. He advised those who were called into the kingdom of Christ being circumcised not to be uncircumcised, and those called in uncircumcision not to be circumcised; the reason he gives is that circumcision is nothing and uncircumcision is nothing (1 Cor. 7:18-19). These ceremonial matters, from a religious viewpoint, were nothing more to Paul than the distinction of sex. If a man wished to follow Jewish customs as a mark of his nationality, Paul had nothing to say against this. So it was a matter of indifference to him to go to the Temple for this rite of purification, whatever it was. It involved no compromise of principle.

This act of Paul's must be understood as the longest step toward peace [between Jewish and Gentile Christians] he knew how to take. No one knew better than he how serious was the tension between the old Jewish and the new Christian principles, but he was not willing to accept the break between Judaism and

Christianity until he had done everything in his power to prevent it. If by publicly going to the Temple he could help heal the breach between Jewish and Gentile Christians, he was ready to go. "Blessed are the peacemakers: for they shall be called the children of God" (Matt. 5:9).

How important is it to accommodate ourselves to those within the Body of Christ whose standards are different from ours? Extremely _____ Important _____ Not important _____

What are the limits of accommodation?

We may ignore Christian principles: Yes _____ No _____

We must hold fast to all of our own persuasions: Yes _____ No _____

We can surrender any point that does not violate our conscience: Yes _____ No _____ Not sure _____

Do I tend to stress the unimportant? Yes _____ No _____ Not sure _____

How flexible and conciliatory am I with different-minded believers without sacrificing my principles? Rate yourself and your local church on the scale below. (1 = inflexible; 7 = very flexible)

Myself   1 2 3 4 5 6 7
Our Local Church   1 2 3 4 5 6 7

Spend some time sharing your ratings in the group.

In verse 25, to what earlier decision regarding Gentile believers did James refer? (See 15:19-20.) _____

Read 21:27-40

Invite the person assigned to tell the story of verses 27-40.

Who was the Gentile they thought Paul had brought into the Temple (v. 29)? _____

In the midst of the turmoil that followed Paul's seizure and arrest, the magnificent dignity of the man shone forth. He asked for permission to speak. With a gesture he calmed the mob. There was no rancor or bitterness, and he was in complete possession of himself as he spoke. Respectful of authority, he did not resist arrest. Even when he informed the Romans of his citizenship, and requested his rights, Paul used but did not abuse his legal rights (cf. 16:37-39).

How did legal authority help Paul at this time (vv. 31-32)? _____

What was Paul's attitude toward government authority? Ask a member to read aloud to the group Rom. 13:1-5.

Read 22:1-21

How did Paul defend himself against the false accusations of the mob?

v. 2 He spoke to them in their own dialect, _____.

v. 3 He pointed out his _____ background and zeal.

vv. 4-5 He told how he had _____ the Christians in Jerusalem and Damascus.

vv. 6-16 He _____ to his conversion and call.

What did the Lord tell Paul to do (v. 10)? _____

Whom did God send to help Paul (v. 12)? _____

What did Ananias tell Paul? _____

v. 13 _____

v. 14 _____

v. 15 _____

v. 16 _____

What direct revelation did God give to Paul in verse 21? _____

Let the member assigned tell the story of verses 22-29.

A Pause for Reflection

Briefly share an insight from this session which is most significant for you. Why is this significant?

How do you plan to implement it in your life this week?

Prayer Time

Turn to the section "My Ministry of Intercessory Prayer."

Spend a few minutes reflecting on the question, "What does the Lord want me to do as a result of this Bible study session?" Identify your continuing ministry of intercession. Return to this list throughout the week.

Conclude the session with sentence prayers for each other, each person praying for the one to his right. Then repeat together the prayer of Francis of Assisi:

> O Lord, our Christ, may we have Thy mind and Thy spirit; make us instruments of Thy peace; where there is hatred, let us sow love; where there is injury, pardon; where there is discord, union; where there is doubt, faith; where there is despair, hope; where there is darkness, light; and where there is sadness, joy.
>
> Divine Master, grant that we may not so much seek to be consoled as to console; to be understood as to understand; to be loved as to love; for it is in giving that we receive; it is in pardoning that we are pardoned; and it is in dying that we are born to eternal life. Amen.

Something to Think About or Do

A suggested verse to memorize: Eph. 6:10

You may also wish to store Francis' prayer in your spiritual memory bank.

Before next week, read Acts 22:30—24:27, using your favorite translation.

In order to cover these two lengthy chapters, assign two members to report to the group the accounts given in:

Acts 23:12-22
Acts 23:23-35

9 God's Providence and Our Responsibility

ACTS 22:30—24:27

Introduction

Does God care for his people? Surely. Does God's care relieve us of the responsibility to use our own best judgment? Of course not.

Acts 23—24 illustrates this truth that God's providence does not cancel the need for human ingenuity in the emergencies of life. There is place both for trusting God and for intelligent planning as we seek to serve God. Paul marshalled his human resources, but beyond these, in the quietness of his soul, he heard God's word, "Be of good cheer."

Opening Prayer

Father, we praise You because You are God—the Infinite One who works in ways that are at times mysterious. But we know that You are at work, even though sometimes only later do we recognize Your sovereign will unfolding in the events.

What is our responsibility in the face of Your promise to work in our lives? This is the big question we need answered from Scripture today as You teach us truths about yourself—and about ourselves. In Your Son's name. Amen.

Review

Spend a few minutes in review. Look back over the past week with the Lord. Did you face some decision where you both asked help from God and followed your own best judgment? Yes ____ No ____ If yes, be prepared to share your experience with the group.

Use the space provided below to write out your responses.

How the Lord Helped	The Human Resources I Used

Scriptural Analysis and Application

Read 22:30—23:11

Why did the commander bring Paul before the Sanhedrin (v. 30)? ___

_____

Why do you think Paul addressed the Sanhedrin as "My brothers" (NIV)?

They were fellow Jews: Yes ____ No ____

Paul himself may have once belonged to the Sanhedrin: Yes ____ No ____

He wanted to gain a favorable hearing: Yes ____ No ____

What do you think Paul meant when he called the high priest a "whitewashed wall" (v. 3, NIV)?

A sham: Yes ____ No ____

A dishonest judge: Yes ____ No ____

Other _____

Did Paul know that he was speaking to the high priest (vv. 4-5)? Yes ____ No ____

Why do you think Paul did not recognize the high priest (v. 5)?

Paul had poor eyesight (see Gal. 4:14-15): Yes ____ No ____

There was a new high priest whom Paul had not known: Yes ____ No ____ Other _____

Write below evidence that Paul respected high office even when occupied by an unworthy man (v. 5). _____

Study Dr. Greathouse's observations regarding Paul's speech before the Sanhedrin (vv. 6-9).

> Paul's keen wit saw a way out of his immediate trouble. In the Sanhedrin he knew there were Pharisees and Sadducees. These two parties were doctrinal opposites. . . . The Pharisees believed in the existence of angels and spirits; the Sadducees did not. So Paul shrewdly cried, "Brethren, I am a Pharisee, the son of a Pharisee: of the hope and resurrection of the dead I am called in question."
>
> Paul spoke the truth. He was being tried because he had preached the hope of Israel—the resurrection from the dead. The central apostolic message was the resurrection of Jesus as God's vindication of Him as the Messiah. But, unintentionally or otherwise, Paul did not mention Jesus. His words about the resurrection drove a division between the two groups and won the goodwill of the Pharisees. The hearing turned into a row.
>
> This lesson underscores the utter humanness of Paul. He loved God; his heart was set on the glory of God; he was willing to suffer and die, if need be; but he was still a human being with feelings and wits. And he used his wits to his own advantage.

Do you think God approved of this action by Paul? Yes ____ No ____ Why? _____

Read together God's promise to Paul: "The following night the Lord stood near Paul and said, 'Take courage! As you have testified about me in Jerusalem, so you must also testify in Rome'" (23:11, NIV).

Read 23:12-35

Ask the person appointed, to tell the story of the plot to kill Paul, and how it was thwarted (23:12-22).

Ask the person appointed to review the account, to tell the story of Paul's transfer to Caesarea (23:23-35).

Review the ways in which God was providentially working in Paul's life.

How did He use Roman soldiers (23:10)? _____

How did He use a young man (23:16-22)? _____

How did He use the Roman commander (vv. 23-24)? _____

Pause for a moment and let group members share times in which they believe God was at work providentially in their lives.

From where did the name *centurion* originate as applied to a Roman army officer (consider v. 23)? _____

What was the name of the Roman commander in Jerusalem (v. 26)?

In his letter to Felix, how do you think Claudius tried to reflect his own conduct in the case?

v. 27: Favorably _____ Unfavorably _____
v. 28: Favorably _____ Unfavorably _____
v. 29: Favorably _____ Unfavorably _____
v. 30: Favorably _____ Unfavorably _____

Trace on the map Paul's route from Jerusalem to Antipatris to Caesarea. How far was the journey? _____

Read 24:1-16

What do you think Tertullus was trying to accomplish in verses 2-4?

What were the charges made against Paul?

v. 5 _____
v. 5 _____
v. 5 _____
v. 6 _____

How did Paul respond to the false accusations?

v. 11 _____
v. 12 _____
v. 13 _____

What admissions did Paul make?

v. 14a _____
v. 14b _____
v. 14c _____
v. 15 _____
v. 16 _____

Study Dr. Greathouse's comments on verses 14-16.

"But this I confess unto thee, that after the way which they call heresy, so worship I the God of my fathers." At the cost of running counter to the orthodox faith of the Jews, Paul explained his personal faith. In the crucible of great soul agony he had found the true worship of God through Jesus. Each person must "buy the truth" for himself. The price he must pay is the same Paul paid: complete abandonment and absolute honesty. Then he will experience the power of Christ. "But we can no more witness to what we have not experienced than we can return from where we have never been." Do I understand this?

Such an experience is Bible-based. Paul could confess: "Believing all things which are written in the law and in the prophets." A dynamic Christian witness finds its basis in the written Word. We must submit our lives to the judgment of that Word, acknowledge that we are sinners—hopelessly and helplessly lost apart from Christ. Then we must believe the Word: "If we confess our sins, he is faithful and just to forgive us our sins, and to cleanse us from all unrighteousness" (1 John 1:9).

Such an experience is God-oriented. Our hope is in God. The Bible is a faithful record, inspired and true; but spiritual life is the gift of the God who brings life out of death! The same power which raised our Lord Jesus out of the grave quickens us from the death of trespasses and sins (Eph. 1:18—2:10).

Finally, such an experience is life-tested. "And herein do I exercise myself, to have always a conscience void of offence toward God, and toward men." To have a witness with power we must have such a conscience.

The need of this hour is for men and women who know firsthand the power of Christ in their lives, who are so Spirit-filled and love-controlled that they will dare to get into trouble for the One who died in their behalf. O God, make me such a man!

Read 24:17-21

How did Paul explain his presence in Jerusalem (v. 17)? _____

How did he defend his presence in the Temple courts (v. 18)?
    He was _____ clean.
    There was no _____ with him.
    He was not involved in any _____.

What elements of a fair trial did Paul point out to be missing?
    v. 19 _____
    v. 20 _____

What slight provocation for the disturbance did Paul acknowledge (v. 21)? _____

Read 24:22-27

Do you think Felix was convinced that Paul was guilty? Yes _____ No _____

What further evidence did Felix suggest (v. 22)? _____

What consideration did the governor show to Paul (v. 23)? _____

Why do you think Felix held a second hearing for Paul (vv. 24-26)?

YES NO

____ ____ To give his wife opportunity to hear the prisoner.

____ ____ Felix himself was influenced toward Christ by Paul's testimony.

____ ____ Felix hoped that Paul would offer him a bribe to free him.

How frustrated do you think Paul felt, held in jail for two years because the judge wanted a bribe to free an innocent man? Terribly ____ Some ____ Little ____ Why? _____

Have you ever had the feeling that everything was falling apart and wondered what the world was coming to? Have you been tempted to imagine God had His back to the wall? What shall we do in these hours?

Let us reaffirm that God is in control. Remember Paul's words, "Jesus Christ is Lord" (Phil. 2:11). Let us remind ourselves that this world and human destiny remain in His hands. He is in charge. He has the game plan and the power to turn things around completely.

With this affirmation clear, let us pray and sometimes fast for our leaders. Let us trust that God himself will provide the guidance needed to correct the injustices. Jesus is Lord of History. The providence of God rules the world. We believe it. Let us act on it.

A Pause for Reflection

Briefly share one insight from this session which is most significant for you. Why is it significant? How do you plan to integrate it into your life this week?

Prayer Time

Turn to the section "My Ministry of Intercessory Prayer."

Spend a few minutes reflecting upon the question, "Is there some seeming injustice in my life that I have found hard to accept? Am I ready to try Christ's formula of faith in Him and forgiveness for the one who has wronged me?"

Would you wish to share the problem with the group, and ask their prayer support?

Conclude the session with prayer, focusing on the needs expressed, and thanking God for Paul's example of Christlike faith and patience.

Something to Think About or Do

Suggested passage to remember: Hab. 3:17-19.

Before next week, read Acts 25:1—26:32.

In order to cover this two-chapter study adequately, ask two persons to study carefully and report to the group the stories in:

Acts 24:27—25:7

Acts 25:13-27

10 Standing Tall

ACTS 25:1—26:32

Introduction

When is a man really free? No one is more a slave, said Goethe, "than he who thinks himself free without being so."

In these chapters, the characteristic thing abut Paul was that he turned his personal defense into a witness for Christ. Bible scholars remind us that the original idea of witnessing is testifying in a law court. A witness is one who can tell of direct and personal experience in which he took part.

Paul was such a witness. He stands tall in his own defense, and as an example to us, who in various contemporary ways are called to defend ourselves and what we believe.

Opening Prayer

Father, again in these chapters we are reminded of the bigness of Paul—the spiritual depths from which he drew when the demands on him were heaviest. We need that strength to be courageous when the pressure is greatest, and the temptation to buckle under is keenest.

Forgive us for our timid Christianity—continually afraid to share our lives and our faith with others.

We are learning from Paul—growing—and becoming more confident in our witness. Thank You, Father, for his witness before King Agrippa, and before us. He stands tall. We want to stand beside him. In Jesus' name. Amen.

Review

Spend a few minutes in review. Look back over the past week with the Lord and reflect upon it. Perhaps you could ask:

What opportunities for ministry can I praise God for?

What answer to prayer?

What do I need to confess? Failure to rise above temporal frustrations? Tendency to retreat under pressure?

What can I share with the group that will build them up in Jesus? Lessons Christ has taught me this week? Insights into God's providence and our responsibility?

Use this space below to write out your responses.

What the Lord Has Done	My Responses: Praise/Confession/Sharing

Scriptural Analysis and Application

Read 25:1-12

Let the person appointed to tell the story, review the events of 24:27—25:7.

Why did the Jews bring up Paul's case for a new hearing at this time (24:27)? _____

What kind of people were wanting to kill Paul (25:2-3)? _____

How would you describe Festus' conduct in the following situations:

vv. 4-5: Fair _____ Courageous _____ Compromising _____
v. 6: Compromising _____ Just _____ Right _____
v. 9: Right _____ Wrong _____ Compromising _____

What three points did Paul make in his defense (v. 8)?

1. _____
2. _____
3. _____

Ask a member to read aloud for the group Paul's response to Festus' request that he go to Jerusalem to stand trial (vv. 10-11).

Paul appealed to Caesar for his trial, but Agrippa told Festus that the Apostle could have been set free if he had not made this appeal.

Was Paul mistaken in making the appeal? Yes _____ No _____ Not sure _____ Why? _____

Ask a member to read aloud for the group Acts 23:11. Do you think this message from God played a part in Paul's decision to make his appeal for a trial in Rome? Yes _____ No _____ Not sure _____

To say that Paul chose the Caesar appeal simply as the means of getting to Rome is to limit God. It is also to ignore the point that being set free could have meant travel not only to Rome, but to Spain and beyond.

Have you ever made a quick decision and later wondered if the decision was correct? Yes _____ No _____

How are we to handle decisions which appear to have no clear-cut direction from the Lord?

_____ Enter open doors
_____ Use our best judgment
_____ Consult with trusted friends
_____ Wait until guidance comes

Read 25:13-27

Ask the person assigned to tell the story of verses 13-27, to give the report at this time.

Agrippa, whose full name was Herod Agrippa II, was a regional ruler in Palestine. Felix, and then Festus, were the Roman governors of this province of the empire. They were the persons directly accountable to Caesar for the government of the territory—as Pilate had been in Jesus' day. Under these Roman governors Herod Agrippa had a measure of authority for local administration; and the Romans permitted him to use the title King Herod. Although Agrippa had no Jewish blood, he was a native to the area. He was thus more acceptable to the Jews than foreign conquerors from Rome. He was also more knowledgeable of Jewish customs and sensitivities.

It was proper protocol for the resident Agrippa and his wife to make a courtesy call on the new Roman governor. It was also natural that the new governor from Rome should seek counsel from the ruling local leader of the province.

Like Felix before him, Festus in his treatment of Paul was careful to abide by Roman _____ (v. 16). Also like Felix, he was _____ _____ (v. 17) in conducting Paul's hearing.

What do you think prompted Agrippa's interest in Paul's case (v. 22)?
Curiosity: Yes _____ No _____
Concern for the Jewish people: Yes _____ No _____
Concern for religious truth: Yes _____ No _____

Read 26:1-18

What courtesy did Paul give to Agrippa (v. 2)? _____
_____

What compliment did Paul pay to the king (v. 3)? _____

What request did Paul make (v. 3)? _____

What do you think was God's promise to which Paul referred in verses
6 and 8? _____

In his earlier life what four kinds of persecution had Paul pressed
against Christ's followers?

v. 10 _____
v. 10 _____
v. 11 _____
v. 11 _____

Ask a member to read aloud for the group Paul's testimony to his
conversion and call (vv. 12-18).

What were the two sources from which Paul was to get his Christian
witness (v. 16)?

1. _____
2. _____

What five results were to occur in the lives of men as a consequence
of Paul's preaching (vv. 17-18)?

1. _____
2. _____
3. _____
4. _____
5. _____

Read 26:19-32

What was Paul's response to Christ's call (v. 19)? _____
_____

To whom did Paul witness (v. 20)?

1. _____
2. _____
3. _____

What three doctrines did Paul preach (v. 20)?

1. _____

2. _____

3. _____

Read together Paul's testimony to Agrippa:

> "I have had God's help to this very day, and so I stand here and testify to small and great alike. I am saying nothing beyond what the prophets and Moses said would happen— that the Christ would suffer and, as the first to rise from the dead, would proclaim light to his own people and to the Gentiles" *(26:22-23, NIV)*.

Paul's witness was that of a changed man. There is no more powerful witness to the reality of God than a transformed life. William Barclay relates the conversion of the evangelist Brownlow North. In his early days he had lived anything but a Christian life. Once just before entering the pulpit to preach, he received a letter which informed him that its writer had evidence of some disgraceful thing North had done before he became a Christian. If North preached, the writer proposed to interrupt the service and tell the whole congregation of the sin.

Brownlow North took the letter into the pulpit and read it to the congregation. He himself told them the thing he had done. Then he testified that while the charge was true, Christ had completely changed him— and could do the same for them.

The proof of the divine power of Christianity is its power to make bad men good. The world can answer our theological arguments; it cannot answer a transformed life.

What do you think made the heathen governor, Festus, believe that Paul was out of his mind (vv. 23-24)? _____

On what basis did Paul think his testimony might seem more reasonable to King Agrippa than to Festus (vv. 26-27)? _____

In verse 27, Paul made a direct appeal to Agrippa to confess his faith in the Christian message. In verse 28 Agrippa responded to Paul's earnest confrontation: "Almost thou persuadest me to be a Christian."

The reply is the basis from which has come the familiar gospel song "Almost Persuaded." Ask a member to read aloud for the group the words of the song.

> *"Almost persuaded" now to believe;*
> *"Almost persuaded" Christ to receive;*
> *Seems now some soul to say,*

"Go, Spirit, go Thy way.
Some more convenient day
    On Thee I'll call."

"Almost persuaded," come, come today.
"Almost persuaded," turn not away.
Jesus invites you here;
Angels are ling'ring near;
Prayers rise from hearts so dear.
    O wand'rer, come!

"Almost persuaded," harvest is past!
"Almost persuaded," doom comes at last!
"Almost" cannot avail;
"Almost" is but to fail!
Sad, sad, that bitter wail,
    "Almost," but lost!

—PHILIP P. BLISS

The NIV translators phrase Agrippa's response as an abrupt rejection of Paul's appeal: "Do you think that in such a short time you can persuade me to be a Christian?"

From reading the account, which attitude do you think Agrippa showed?

Sincere interest: Yes _____ No _____
Cynical response: Yes _____ No _____

How do you evaluate Paul's reply to Agrippa (v. 29)?

Effective witness: Yes _____ No _____ Not sure _____
Simply ending the conversation: Yes _____ No _____
Sincere expression of concern: Yes _____ No _____

A Pause for Reflection

Briefly share with the group one insight from this session which is most significant for you. Why is it significant?

_____

_____

How do you plan to implement it in your life this week?

_____

Prayer Time

Turn to the section "My Ministry of Intercessory Prayer."

Spend a few minutes reflecting on the question, "What does the Lord want me to do in the area of witnessing?" Ponder this question through the week. Be specific—write down the who, where, and how.

Conclude the session with group prayer, focusing on the need for witnessing represented in your prayer lists.

Something to Think About or Do

Suggested verse to memorize—Acts 26:29.

Prepare a written testimony. Tell about your life before you became a Christian, how you became a Christian, and your life since becoming a Christian.

Share your testimony with another group member before sharing it with a non-Christian.

Before next week, read Acts 27:1-44.

Assign three members of the group to represent: Aristarchus, the ship's captain, and the centurion. Let each one report the story from his point of view. Encourage them to use creative imagination, but within the limits of the facts given in Acts 27. Be sure that each one tells how he was influenced by Paul.

Ask the person representing the ship's captain to be prepared to tell the stories in 27:27-32, and in verses 39-44.

11   Great Faith Makes Great Men

ACTS 27:1-44

Introduction

Although Paul did not write this contemporary gospel song, it could well have been his testimony. Read the words as an introduction to the study of this chapter.

Peace in the Midst of the Storm

When the world that I've been living in collapses at my feet,
    When my life is shattered and torn,
Tho' I'm windswept and battered I can cling to His cross,
    And find peace in the midst of the storm.

When in twenty-four short hours, years of living are brought to moments;
    And when life's final picture is taking form;
In the dark room of my suffering there's a light shining through;
    He gives me peace in the midst of my storm.

When my body has been broken 'til it's wracked in misery,
    When all the doctors shake their heads and look forlorn;
Jesus comes to make my bedside a cathedral of hope and love;
    He sends His peace right into the midst of my storm.

CHORUS:
There is peace in the midst of my storm-tossed life;
    Oh, there's an Anchor, there's a Rock to cast my faith upon;
Jesus rides in my vessel, so I'll fear no alarm;
    He gives me peace in the midst of my storm. *

—STEPHEN ADAMS

The purpose of our study this week is to emphasize the necessity and nature of Christian faith and courage. In spite of our best efforts, we sometimes find ourselves threatened with destruction. How we react in such crises reveals the depth and nature of our faith.

Opening Prayer

Father, we are discovering through our study of Paul, that those who know God best have great thoughts about God. We really want to know You better.

As we study Paul's journey to Rome, teach us about Your nature and character. Teach us to think greater thoughts about You. In so doing, may we find great faith which makes great men and women. Through Christ our Lord. Amen.

Review

Spend a few minutes in review. Look back over the past week with the Lord and reflect upon it. Perhaps you could ask:

What storm has God brought me through in the past year? How have I been blessed by the faith and courage of some other Christian?

What do I need to confess? Failure to appreciate God's help? The need to encourage another by recognizing his gifts?

Use the space provided below to write out your responses.

What the Lord Has Done	My Responses: Praise/Confession/Sharing

Scriptural Analysis and Application

Retrace the events in Acts 27 (cf. NIV) with a map. (See "The Mediterranean World in the Time of Paul" in this study guide.) Let one person lead

the group, while others follow on their own maps and make notes. Describe
what happened at the following points on Paul's journey to Rome.

Caesarea (25:13; 27:1)   Salmone (v. 7)
Sidon (v. 3)   Fair Havens (v. 8)
Cyprus (v. 4)   Lasea (v. 8)
Cilicia (v. 5)   Phoenix (v. 12)
Pamphylia (v. 5)   Cauda (v. 16)
Myra (v. 5)   Adriatic Sea (v. 27)
Cnidus (v. 7)   Malta (28:1)
Crete (v. 7)

Read 27:1-12

Adramyttium (v. 2), the home port of the ship, lay at the head of an
inlet of the Aegean Sea, about 75 miles east of Troas (see map).

Who was Aristarchus, and why would he have been on this trip with
Paul (Acts 19:29; 20:4)? _____

Let the person representing Aristarchus give his report at this point.

What friends do you think Paul might have had in Sidon (v. 3)? _____
_____

Have you ever been helped by the kindness of fellow Christians in a
strange place? Yes _____ No _____ If so, be prepared to share the experience.

Why do you think it was necessary to change ships at Myra (vv. 5-6)?
_____

In verse 9 the "Fast" refers to the Jewish Day of Atonement which
occurred at the time of the year when storms were expected in the Mediterranean Sea.

In verse 10, do you think Paul's warning came from divine revelation,
or from his experience as a sea traveler? _____

Why do you think the centurion took the advice of the ship's captain
instead of the advice of Paul (vv. 11-12)? _____

Let the person representing the centurion give his report at this time.

Read 27:13-26

Why did the captain leave Fair Havens when he did (v. 13)? _____
_____

Why were they unable to make it to the harbor at Phoenix (vv.
14-15)? _____
_____

In what direction did the storm drive the ship (vv. 15-16)? _____

What emergency actions indicate the ferocity of the storm?
    v. 17 _____
    v. 18 _____
    v. 19 _____
How long did the storm last (vv. 20, 33)? _____
Describe Paul's attitude at the worst point in the storm:
    v. 21 _____
    v. 22 _____
    vv. 23-24 _____
What promise did God give Paul regarding other persons on board (v. 24)? _____

Pause and reflect upon your response to things that do not go the way you expect. Finish this sentence: My typical response is _____
_____
_____

Compare your response with others in the group. What can we learn from Paul about peace in the midst of our storms?
    1. _____
    2. _____

Read the following quote from Dr. Greathouse.

Let us begin where we should—with that marvelous declaration: "God, whose I am, and whom I serve" (27:23). Christian faith is *God-centered*. God is an End in himself. He is to be served because He is God. He does not need us; we need Him. He is not a prop we are to put under our sagging civilization or our sick personalities; He is the Hub around whom all life should revolve.

Paul served God; we want God to serve us. Quite unconsciously we assume that God exists especially for our benefit. We have outgrown an earth-centered astronomy; we have not laid aside a man-centered theology. The tragedy is that, while our science is making rapid strides, our faith is going in reverse. We say, "We must have a revival to save Western civilization." If we do not have a revival, Western civilization may not long be worth saving! But God does not send revivals to perpetuate our pride; we need a revival because of who God is and what we are. We need a revival because our sins are a grief to God, because we are dishonoring God, because we have forgotten God.

We say, "You should confess your sins and commit your life to Christ, so you will have peace of mind." This is also an ego-centric approach. You should confess your sins and turn from them for the same reason America should repent—for the glory of God. This was Paul's faith. God was not a crutch for Paul; He was his Creator and Controller.

To what degree do you believe the following statements:
    (1 = very much; 7 = not at all)

1. God is the Supreme Reality in the world.   1 2 3 4 5 6 7

2. God controls the destiny of men and nations.   1 2 3 4 5 6 7

3. Although we are free, God is able to override human choices and Satan's maneuvers to make all things work together for the good of them that love Him.   1 2 3 4 5 6 7

Recall the most difficult experience of your life when God brought you safely through. Be prepared to share your testimony.

Read 27:27-44

Let the person chosen to represent the ship's captain tell the story of 27-32, 39-44 and report how he was influenced by Paul.

In addition to Paul's confidence in God, he used common sense. Read verse 33. In the vessel about to be broken to pieces on the rocks, Paul insisted that everybody eat a good meal. Barclay comments:

He did not have the slightest doubt that God would do His part but he also knew that men must do theirs. It could never be said of Paul as it is said of some people that they were so heavenly minded they were of no earthly good.[1]

Look at some critical issue currently facing you. What are some common-sense activities you could do to alleviate some pain and hurt within yourself? In others? Ask the group members for support and additional suggestions.

What did Paul do in verse 35 to reflect his faith in God? _____

_____

What effect did Paul's faith and courage have on his companions (v. 36)? _____

One Christian writes:

We don't have problems talking about the sufficiency of God; to radically depend on Him to meet our every need is quite a different matter.

A Pause for Reflection

Ask one member to read aloud for the group, Rom. 8:28-39.

Briefly share with the group one insight from this session which is most significant for you.

Prayer Time

Turn to the section "My Ministry of Intercessory Prayer."

Spend a few minutes reflecting upon the questions, "What witness of love and care, what acts of love and encouragement, or what ministries of service does God want me to do or say this week?" Be specific. Write down the who, where, and how.

Conclude the session with a prayer for courage, faith, and faithfulness.

Something to Think About or Do

Suggested verses to memorize: Hab. 3:17-19.

During the week review the great hymns of the Church to catch a new vision of the majesty and faithfulness of God. Begin with hymns like "Holy, Holy, Holy," "Great Is Thy Faithfulness," "God Will Take Care of You," and "How Firm a Foundation."

After reviewing these great hymns, write your own hymn or paragraph of praise and thanksgiving to God. Be prepared to share it with the group at the next session.

Using your favorite translation, read in preparation for next week's study, Acts 28:1-31.

12 The Continuing Mission

ACTS 28:1-31

Introduction

At the height of his Salvation Army ministry, Samuel Logan Brengle was struck on the head by a brick hurled by some dissident. For 18 months he was confined to his home. During that time he began to write his classic little book, *Helps to Holiness*. A new ministry was born that is still meeting the needs of Christian people. Near the end of his enforced confinement Mrs. Brengle brought that brick to him. Upon it she had inscribed these words, "You meant it for evil, but God meant it for good."

So were the years of Paul's confinement in Rome. This study of Acts 28 reminds us anew that God knows how to make all things work together for good to them that love Him. He is the sovereign Lord of history.

God brought Paul to the capital city for a special mission—"to testify in Rome about me." The fulfillment of that mission is beautifully portrayed in the closing verses of Acts. "For two whole years Paul stayed there in his own rented house and welcomed all who came to see him. Boldly and without hindrance he preached the kingdom of God and taught about the Lord Jesus Christ" (28:30-31, NIV).

May this concluding chapter of Acts spark new ministries for us as we commit ourselves to continue the mission Paul began—to use our gifts in our setting, personalizing the call of Jesus to "go . . . into all the world, and preach the gospel to every creature" (Mark 16:15).

Opening Prayer

Father, we come to the close of this study with thanksgiving. We are thankful for the opportunity to see Your Holy Spirit at work in Paul's missionary journeys. We have discovered people who loved You. We have found life experiences filled with human drama. We have received a new challenge, a new hope, a new reason for being.

We confess our deep desire to have an effective ministry in our circum-

stances as Paul had in his. You have heard our prayers, and You are teaching us new truths about ourselves and about Your mission in the world through us.

Thank You, Father, for these promptings in our lives. We needed them—and we are grateful. In Jesus' name. Amen.

Review

Spend a few minutes in review. Look back over the past three months with the Lord and reflect upon them.

> What have I learned that I praise God for? What new opportunities for ministry has the Holy Spirit shown me?
>
> What new friends have I found in our group? What have they done to build me up in my faith? How should I thank them for their ministry to me?

Use the space provided below to write your answers.

What the Lord Has Done	My Responses: Praise/Sharing
What Christian Friends Have Done	My Responses: Praise/Sharing

Scriptural Analysis and Application

Divide the class into three small groups. Ask group No. 1 to study and report on Acts 28:1-10, showing Paul's dealing with the people of Malta. Group No. 2 will read verses 12-15 and report Paul's attitude toward the Christians of Rome. Let group No. 3 read verses 16-31 and outline Paul's message to the Jews.

Read 28:1-10

Let group No. 1 give their report on verses 1-10.

How far had the storm driven the ship (see map)? _____

What kindness did the islanders show the shipwrecked travelers (v. 2)?

_____

What characteristics of Paul do you see in verse 3a? _____

In verse 4, what moral law is reflected in the thinking of these heathen people? _____

Who was the chief official of Malta (v. 7)? _____

How did Paul minister to the family of Publius (v. 8)? _____

_____

Have you ever experienced a case of divine healing in yourself or in another? Yes _____ No _____. If yes, be prepared to tell of your experience.

How did the islanders respond to Paul's ministry (v. 10)?

        1. _____

        2. _____

Read 28:11-15

Ask group No. 2 for their report.

How long did Paul's party stay on the island of Malta (v. 11)? _____

_____

What was the home port of the ship on which they sailed from Malta to Puteoli (v. 11)? _____

On the map, trace their journey:

                        Malta

                        Syracuse

                        Rhegium

                        Puteoli

How far did they travel on the ship (use the scale of miles on your map)? _____

In verses 14-15, whom do you think Luke meant by "the brothers" (NIV)? _____

How do you think Paul's party traveled from Puteoli to Rome? ____

___

Why do you think Paul thanked God when he saw the "brothers" from Rome (v. 15)? _____

In a revival meeting a member of the church board testified: "I am encouraged in the Lord."

What do you think he meant? _____

Read 28:16-29

Let group No. 3 report.

What were Paul's living accommodations in Rome (v. 16)?

1. _____
2. _____

What was Paul's first order of business, once settled in Rome (v. 17)?

___

What facts did Paul tell the Jewish leaders?

v. 17 _____

v. 17 _____

v. 17 _____

v. 18 _____

v. 18 _____

v. 19 _____

What reason did Paul give to explain his imprisonment (v. 20)? ____

___

What was the response of the Jewish leaders in Rome?

v. 21 _____

v. 21 _____

v. 22 _____

v. 22 _____

What was the subject of Paul's message (v. 23)? _____

What two sources did Paul use to try to persuade the Jews that Jesus was the Messiah (v. 23)?

1. _____
2. _____

What was the response to Paul's preaching (vv. 24-25)?

1. _____
2. _____

What was Paul's closing statement to those who refused to accept the message (vv. 26-28)? _____

Verses 26-27 are a quotation from the prophet Isaiah. Do you think the Jews in Rome would be more likely to accept Isaiah's condemnation than to accept condemnation from Paul? Yes _____ No _____ Why? _____

God had kept His promise to bring Paul to Rome, and had given him many opportunities both on the way and in Rome to bear witness to Jesus Christ.

Discuss the fact that although God intended for Paul to get to Rome (Acts 23:11), it was not a straight line, and it did not happen immediately.

Include in your discussion the fact that fulfillment of God's promise took Paul through:
1. arrest
2. imprisonment
3. repeated hearings and court trials
4. shipwreck
5. other lengthy delays

Read 28:30-31

During these two years in prison, Paul wrote the Epistles of Philippians, Colossians, Ephesians, and Philemon. What else did he do (Phil. 1:13)?

What was the apparent result of this witness (Phil. 4:21-22)? _____

Who was with Paul in Rome (Phil. 1:1)? _____

What visitors did he have while there?

Eph. 6:21 _____

Col. 4:10 _____

Phil. 4:18 _____

Paul never lost his concern for the congregations he founded and the Christians he nurtured.

Let a member read aloud to the group Paul's prayer for the church at Philippi, written during this time in prison (Phil. 1:3-11).

An Unfinished Book

In the very nature of the case, the Book of Acts must remain unfinished. Remember the widening circle of the Christian mission from Pentecost to Paul's prison ministry in Rome. Rome symbolizes "the uttermost part of the earth" (1:8).

The opening verse of Acts suggests this unfinished assignment: "The former treatise have I made, O Theophilus, of all that Jesus *began* both to do and teach" (italics added). The unmistakable implication is that, in Acts, Luke was recounting some of the things Jesus was continuing to do through the Church. This ministry will not be complete until Christ returns.

Dr. Greathouse writes:

Alexander Irvine tells of his mother, Anna, a poor Irish peasant. One day a neighbor came to her for comfort. Anna took her into the bedroom and said simply, "Just tell Him to lay His hand on your tired head in token that He's with you in your distress." The prayer was answered. The woman said she had received God's comfort. "And did you feel God's hand?" Anna asked. "Yes," was the answer, "but it felt strangely like your hand, Anna." "Yes, the hand was mine," Anna replied, "but it was God's hand, too. God takes a hand wherever He can find it. Sometimes He takes the hand of a bishop, or the hand of a doctor, and sometimes He takes the hand of a poor old creature like me. God takes a hand wherever He can find it."

You and I are the Body of Christ. His ministry of love and salvation He seeks to continue through us. As long as there is one lost soul, He will continue to minister. Will we give Him our bodies?

> Christ has no hands but our hands
> To do His work today;
> He has no feet but our feet
> To lead men in His way;
> He has no tongues but our tongues
> To tell them how He died;
> He has no help but our help
> To bring men to His side.
>
> —ANNIE JOHNSON FLINT

A Pause for Reflection

Spend these moments reflecting on the most significant insights you have received from this study of Acts 13—28. List a few:

1. _____
2. _____
3. _____

How do you plan to incorporate them into your life? _____

Prayer Time

Turn once more to the section "My Ministry of Intercessory Prayer."

Spend a few minutes reflecting on the question, "What prayer concerns from this Bible study does the Lord want me to continue?"

Conclude this final session with sentence prayers. Let all who wish to participate express their feelings of:

Gratitude for the Bible	Requests for courage and faithfulness
Praise for God's love	Intercession for another in the group
Thanks for the Christian fellowship	

Something to Think About or Do

Suggested verse to memorize—John 20:21

MY MINISTRY

WHAT DOES THE LORD
WANT ME TO DO?

OF INTERCESSORY PRAYER

SPECIFIC APPLICATION OF THE WORD TO MINISTRY OPPORTUNITIES

DATE OF ENTRY	MY MINISTRY OF INTERCESSION: SPECIFIC PEOPLE, CONCERNS, NEEDS I WANT TO LIFT TO THE FATHER.	MY WITNESS OF LOVE AND CARE: ACTS OF LOVE, ENCOURAGEMENT, AND MINISTRIES OF SERVICE. WHAT DOES GOD WANT ME TO DO OR SAY? BE SPECIFIC. INCLUDE THE WHEN, WHO, WHERE, AND HOW.

Reference Notes

LESSON 1

1. John Wesley, *Explanatory Notes upon the New Testament* (New York: Eaton & Mains, n.d.), 313-14.

LESSON 4

1. Garry Friesen, *Decision Making and the Will of God* (Portland, Oreg.: Multnomah Press, 1980), 226.

LESSON 6

1. James Garlow, *Partners in Ministry* (Kansas City: Beacon Hill Press of Kansas City, 1981), 94-100.

LESSON 11

1. William Barclay, *The Acts of the Apostles,* in *The Daily Study Bible* (Philadelphia: Westminster Press, 1953), 204.

Write for information about additional individual or small-group Bible study guides to:

Beacon Hill Press of Kansas City
Box 527, Kansas City, MO 64141

NOTES:

NOTES:

NOTES: